# Industrial Demand for Water

**L.S.E. research monographs 3**

This series is published jointly with the London School of Economics and Political Science. It aims to make available research of originality and quality from the whole range of the social sciences, including all the fields and disciplines which are studied at the School. The intention is to provide a continuing outlet for serious scholarly work, and relatively quick publication. The books will be of interest to specialists in the various fields, irrespective of whether they are in universities, government departments, industries or elsewhere, as well as to libraries throughout the world.

Each monograph will be introduced with a foreword by a distinguished authority on the subject, whose aim will be to set the particular research in to the wider framework of the appropriate discipline. Forthcoming monographs include the following:

Changes in Subject Choice at School and University
Celia M. Phillips
The Criminal Liability of Corporations in English Law
L. H. Leigh
The Politics of Decontrol of Industry: Britain and the United States
Susan Armitage
The Administrative Functions of the French Conseil d'Etat
Nancy Rendell
The Concept of Responsibility in the Criminal Law
F. G. Jacobs
Six Studies of Indian Industry
Angus Hone

# Industrial demand for water: a study of South East England

## Judith Anne Rees

With a Preface by C. I. Jackson
of the London School of Economics

London School of Economics and Political Science

Weidenfeld and Nicolson
5 Winsley Street London W1

© 1969 by Judith Anne Rees

SNB 297 17916 0
Printed in Great Britain by
Lowe & Brydone (Printers) Ltd., London.

# Contents

# Tables

# Maps and diagrams

# Symbol key

$a$ = regression constant term
$b, c, d, e$ = regression coefficients
$Q$ = Quantity of water purchased from local undertakings
$QA$ = Quantity of water privately abstracted
$Qt$ = Quantity of water taken in total
$E$ = Number of persons employed
$T$ = Tonnage of raw materials used
$A$ = Age of firm (i.e.: length of time located on present site)
$P$ = Price paid for all purchased supplies per 1000g
$P_m$ = Price paid for metered supplies per 1000 g
$C$ = Cost of abstraction per 1000g
$D$ = Dummy variable
$R_w$ = Rank given to water in a firm's locational decision
$\%L$ = Percentage of labour costs in total cost
$\%M$ = Percentage of raw material costs in total cost
$\%P$ = Percentage of power costs in total cost
$\%T$ = Percentage of transport costs in total cost
$mgd$ = Millions of gallons per day
$mgy$ = Millions of gallons per year
$gpd$ = Gallons per day
$gpy$ = Gallons per year

# Acknowledgements

As much of this work is based on the results of a sample survey, it could not have been completed without the co-operation of the many factory managers who kindly answered the postal questionnaire and allowed me to interview them. In addition I would like to thank the water undertaking and river authority engineers, who have supplied some of the other basic information.

I am extremely grateful for the guidance and criticisms of Dr C. I. Jackson, who has maintained a close interest in every stage of the study. My husband has given me much valuable assistance especially in the more economic and statistical sections of the work. He has also had the unenviable task of reading the many drafts and suggesting improvements. In addition, thanks are due to my fellow graduates in the Senior Laboratory, Geography Department, London School of Economics, 1965-7, from whom I learnt much.

The research would not have been possible without the University of London Bursary and Studentship held for two years from October 1965, and without the generous grant given to me by the Central Research Fund.

# Preface

Perhaps the best tribute to the water supply industry in Britain has been the lack of interest which has been aroused in its activities. For most of us the supply of unlimited water of excellent quality at the turn of a tap has been taken for granted. Those who fought to establish the supply of cheap and pure water on a national scale (including reformers such as Edwin Chadwick and John Stuart Mill) laid the foundations of a major public service.

In recent years, however, there have been signs of growing public concern and occasional dissatisfaction with water supply. The increasing demand for water, which is closely correlated with a rising standard of living, has forced water engineers to seek major new sources of supply. Where this has involved the construction of surface reservoirs, opposition has often been aroused on amenity and other grounds: in the Lake District, Wales, Teesdale and elsewhere. Such new sources are also more expensive to develop than water which was near at hand and the cost of development, combined with the need to renew outmoded equipment, has frequently led to rises in water prices.

On the national scale, two recent developments in water management and control have been of major importance. The first of these has been the trend towards the creation of larger supply authorities. In part this has been caused by the need for cooperation in the development of distant and expensive sources of water; in part also it has been due to the need to ensure that water resources are administered by highly qualified engineers, chemists and other professional staffs. The *Water (Scotland) Act* 1967 transferred the work of 199 statutory suppliers to 13 regional boards. In England and Wales similar amalgamation has been taking place more gradually but no less certainly. Secondly there has been a recognition of the need to consider water as a resource with a variety of alternative uses, which need careful planning if maximum use of the water is to be obtained. On the local scale, for example, several supply authorities have acted to increase the amenity and recreational opportunities provided by their reservoirs and gathering grounds. On a national scale the *Water Resources Act* 1963 created in England and Wales a network of 27 river authorities, which were charged with overall responsibility for water resource development and conservation in their areas. It established also the Water Resources Board to coordinate the activities of the river authorities and to help in determining national policy for water.

Because water supply raised few problems in the past, little attention was paid to the collection of data on needs for water, its uses and its availability. Research on these matters was also comparatively rare and, as with data collection, was essentially local rather than national in character. The river authorities and the Water Resources Board are attempting to remedy these deficiencies and this research monograph is a further contribution. The relatively large sample of firms on which this survey is based enables a more detailed analysis of industrial water use than has been possible in Britain before. In particular, Mrs Rees investigates the relationships between the quantity of water taken by different types of industry and such features as the number of employees and the quantity of raw materials used. The close association which she frequently establishes between water use and such factors will be of value in providing yardsticks for water conservation by individual firms and for predicting future needs.

One feature of water use, particularly by industry, is not shared to the same extent by the other public utilities with which water supply is often classed. A large part of the water used by industry is taken from its source directly by the consumer. Industry does make considerable use of 'piped' water, but it also abstracts vast quantities from surface and subsurface sources directly for its own needs. A feature of this monograph is the way in which public and private supplies are considered separately, both in their relative importance in different industries and in the different uses within individual plants.

Although the sample of firms is drawn from southeast England, the study and its conclusions should be helpful to water authorities, industrialists and regional planners throughout Britain and in other highly industrialised countries. In the diverse 'industry-mix' of the Southeast, it is chiefly the older and heavier types of enterprise which are under-represented. Industrial expansion, whether in southeast England or elsewhere, usually involves industries of the lighter type and this analysis of water requirements by different industry groups will be of value in assisting the orderly development of water resources to meet such expansion.

The research which is described in this monograph is part of a continuing programme of study of water resource problems at the London School of Economics. In introducing it, it is a pleasure also to welcome Judith Rees on her return to the School as she joins the staff of the Department of Geography.

C. I. Jackson

# Chapter 1

# Introduction

### Research aims

The industrial use of water has been a neglected subject in the literature of economic geography and of water supply. In Britain the neglect is at least partly explained by the paucity of published statistics on industrial water consumption. Manufacturers normally obtain their supplies by purchase from statutory water undertakings, or by private abstraction from surface or ground water sources. Some details about the quantity of water supplied by statutory undertakings are available in the *Water Engineers' Handbook* (59[1]), and since 1961 in *Water Statistics* (57.), but these sources of information by no means provide a complete areal coverage of all statutory suppliers. Most undertakings use two different methods of charging consumers for their water supply. Metered water is sold on a quantity basis with the consumer paying for each 1000 gallons used: this type of supply is normally given to industrial and agricultural concerns. An unmetered water supply is usually provided for domestic and most commercial consumers; each of these users is entitled to a supply after payment of an initial charge (the water rate); no record is kept of the quantity of water taken by each customer.[2] Although most authorities do now provide separate information on the quantities of water supplied by meter ' . . . separate records of metered and unmetered supply were not available for any earlier period than 1957 and in the case of many undertakings than 1959' (127 p 94). In addition no published sources provide a breakdown of metered supply into that taken by industrial and agricultural users. Although such information may be available in the records of some undertakings, many others do not make any attempt to subdivide their metered supply. A further difficulty in finding the quantity of water purchased by manufacturing industry is that some firms in some areas are given an unmetered supply and are charged a water rate based on the rateable value of their premises.

   Information on the past and present use by industry of water abstracted from private sources is even more fragmentary. Only after the abstraction licences, introduced by Part IV of the 1963 *Water Resources Act* (119 p 23) have been fully analysed will it be known how much water is being used by manufacturers from private sources. No published statistics exist which are gathered from the industrial consumers themselves and therefore it is not accurately known which industries take how much water for what purposes. Such information is already collected in the United States as one section of the *Census of Manufactures* (129).

Without such data no definitive statements can be made on, for example, future industrial demands for water, or the characteristics of water users, on the possible effects of resource planning and controls, or on the influence of water as a location factor. It is, however, by no means uncommon to find definite statements on all these topics in the water supply literature (43 p iii), (6 p 476), (48 p 153).

The absence of collected information on industrial water consumption has made inevitable the essentially descriptive nature of much of this monograph, since a large proportion of the research work consisted of basic data collection. This obviously cannot be a definitive study of industrial water usage in the whole of Britain; such a task would be beyond the scope of any individual and would be more appropriate to a census collection agency. It was, therefore, decided to confine the study to south east England, an area where water shortages have become quite severe. In fact it has been estimated that to equate the demand from all types of water users with the developed supply within this region an expenditure of some £850 millions will be required between the years 1966 and 2001 (127 p 13).

After a discussion of the methods of analysis and data collection used, and of the characteristics of the 'study area' an economic evaluation of the water supply industry will be attempted. Industrial water usage cannot be treated in isolation from the other competing demands for the resource. Economic supplies of water are limited and so competition between users does occur, and this will become accentuated if developed supplies are not extended in keeping with demand increases. It will therefore be necessary to discuss in brief the economic characteristics of some non-industrial water consumers, and to examine the position of industrial demand in the competitive market.

The central chapters of the work contain an analysis of the uses to which manufacturing industry puts water, the sources from which the demand for water is satisfied, and the factors which determine the quantity of water taken by firms in the various industry groups. These will be followed by a consideration of the influence of water on industrial location. Possible future trends in industrial demands for water and in water's position as a location factor will then be discussed in Chapter 6, and this chapter will also contain the main conclusions and implications of the study.

## Statistical sources and methods of analysis
### 1  *The 'Industrial Survey'*
The primary data source was a postal questionnaire survey sent out during
the spring and summer of 1966, to a random sample of manufacturers
which are located in the south east. Firms employing under 15 persons were
omitted from the sample since they play a negligible part in the region's
water economy. A sample frame including the total population of firms
located within the 'study area' was devised from the Kompass *Register*[3]
(75), which is the most complete of the accessible industrial directories.
Three small test areas were chosen to assess the accuracy of the Kompass
listing; the areas studied were the Medway towns, Bishop's Stortford and
East Grinstead. Known complete lists of firms within the test areas were
compared with those recorded in Kompass.[4] It was found that three types
of manufacturing units were under-represented: (a) firms with under ten
employees, (b) firms or plants which have been established more recently
than January, 1965, and (c) branch plants. The under-representation of the
small firms does not affect the survey sample frame, since all firms
employing less than fifteen persons would have been excluded in any case.
Under-representation of firms established more recently than January 1965
was expected since there is an inevitable time lag before new firms are
surveyed and added to the current *Register*. This does mean, however,
that the survey results are strictly applicable only to firms established
before 1965; any new demand trends established subsequent to this date
will not emerge. Although the sample frame (i.e. Kompass) did include
the vast majority of manufacturing firms, it was found that some branch
plants were not recorded in their respective areas, but were listed under
their head offices, which were usually located in the Greater London
Council area. If a firm's headquarters are located within the 'study area',
the lack of separate listings for branch plants does not affect the sample
as the survey was conducted on the basis of individual firms; separate
forms were not sent to each plant. The selected sample firms were
requested to complete the questionnaire for their largest plant located in
the south east, although space was allowed for the firm to comment on
any special water demands in any of the smaller branches. In this way it
was hoped that the results would be comparable as the surveyed units
would not sometimes be single plants and sometimes multi-branch firms
(19 p 4). It would appear to be the case that the majority of non-recorded
branch plants in the 'study area' do have their main plant or an office
within the south east. In fact, in the three test areas, no case emerged
where the non-recorded branch plant had its headquarters listed as outside

the south east. It is, however, conceivable that some such plants have been excluded from the sample frame, but it is not thought that this will bias materially the survey results.[5]

After the sample frame had been tested for completeness, it was stratified into 15 industry groups, as shown in Appendix A. The industrial classification used had to be closely based on that used in the Kompass *Register*, which means that it was not possible to obtain homogeneous water using characteristics within each industrial stratum. Groups containing firms which vary greatly in their demands for and uses of water could not be disaggregated. This was especially the case in the plastics and rubber industry and in the non-metallic minerals group. Some of the Kompass industry groups were omitted as they contained non-manufacturing units, and others were combined. The combination of industries was designed to reduce the size of the sample needed to ensure that sufficient replies would be obtained in each industrial stratum. To avoid large variations within groups only industries with similar water using characteristics were combined.[6] For example, precision and electrical engineering firms were formed into one group, and mechanical and transport engineering concerns into another. It was not possible to use the *Standard Industrial Classification* as it differs from that used in Kompass, nor would it have been a useful one for this particular study as similarity of water using characteristics was not one of the criteria used in devising this classification (122).

The next stage was to calculate the number of firms to be selected randomly from each industry group. Sampling errors in the results will be greatest when the industry group contains firms with dissimilar water using characteristics (i.e. the standard deviation in the quantity of water used will be high). On the other hand the error is smaller the higher the proportion of the total population which is sampled (89 p 115) (39 pp 169-83). Therefore, groups with high standard deviations need a larger number of observations than relatively homogeneous ones, if the sampling errors are to be kept roughly the same over the industries. As British statistics are not available from which to calculate the standard deviation in the quantity of water taken within each industry group, it was thought that the use of American data would provide a rough guide. In the United States *Census of Manufactures*, the average quantity of water used is given for firms within each minimum list heading (i.e. subdivisions of the industry groups, for example the food industry is divided into 38 subgroups including jam manufacture, ice cream production and so on) (129 vol 1 Sect 11). It was, therefore, possible to aggregate the figures into the fifteen industry groups used in this study, and to calculate an approximate standard deviation for each.[7] Although it was expected that the standard deviation of water usage is likely to be much greater in the United States than in south east England, reflecting the more diverse conditions, it was thought that the relative standard deviations between industry groups are similar. For example, from the American data it would appear that firms in the chemical and paper industries vary greatly in the quantity of water demanded; in other words their standard deviations are high. On the other hand it was found that the standard deviations in the engineering groups are low. It is likely that in Britain the relative size of the standard deviations between these industry groups will be similar. The American standard deviations were then used to obtain the number of firms to be sampled within each industry group[8] and the estimation errors that would occur if this number of firms was sampled was found from the formula, $d(\text{error}) = 2S/n_h$. Some redistribution of sample numbers was then necessary to obtain similar sampling errors in each industry group, and to obtain sufficient observations in some of the smaller groups. The number of firms finally sampled in each industrial stratum is shown in Appendix A.

The questionnaire, which was sent out to the randomly selected firms is reproduced as Appendix B. To facilitate computations the questionnaire was laid out and the questions were framed in such a way that the replies could be directly transferred on to punch cards (24 pp 1-10). In an attempt to improve the overall response rate, firms for which water was of no importance at all in their locational decision or in their production were asked to complete only the first part of the survey form. It was thought that many such firms would not be prepared to complete a lengthy questionnaire on a subject which had no bearing on their own production. The completion of part of the form would at least give some insight into the locational decision, and it would also point out the characteristics of firms for which water was an unimportant consideration. Three reminders were sent out at monthly intervals in an attempt to increase the number of respondents, but the improvement was marginal after the first reminder. Firms that had gone into liquidation (3 in number) or had moved out of the south east (2) were replaced by new sample firms. Manufacturers with only warehousing or office premises in the study area were also replaced, although in the later stages of the survey replacement was not attempted in order to complete the study within the allotted time. Visits were made to some of the firms, either, if the firm requested this, or because the answers given to the questionnaire were unusual or were obviously inaccurate. In addition, a number of firms (40) were randomly selected for interviewing in order to examine the reasoning behind the replies.

In total 600 questionnaires were sent out, although non-replacement of storage and office premises towards the end of the survey period reduced the size of the sample for all practical purposes to 585 firms. The questionnaire was returned by 261 firms, of which 253 were found to be usable; an overall usable response rate of 43% was therefore obtained. This rate was relatively low despite the reminders, but was probably to be expected given the specialized nature of the inquiry. The number of firms positively refusing to answer the questionnaire was high, accounting for 15.5% of the sampled firms. Refusals were especially common in the drink, textiles, paper and chemical groups, all of which are relatively large water-using industries. Many firms expressed an unwillingness to give details of their water consumption, because they felt such information might enable rivals to deduce their manufacturing techniques. Another common reason for refusal was the non-availability of time or staff to complete the form or to hold interviews. There was a tendency for firms in which water was of no importance at all to ignore the questionnaire rather than refuse to answer it. Appendix A, Column 5, shows that the usable response rate varies greatly between industry groups, which has meant that some combination of groups was inevitable to obtain statistically significant results in the regression analysis on the quantity of water taken by firms.

The information derived from the sample survey was classified and tabulated by computer using a single digit tabulation programme (81). Simple and multiple least squares regression was the main method of analysis although some use was made also of frequency distributions and histograms.

## 2 Abstraction licences

A second important source of information was the *Licence of Right Registers* kept by the river authorities in south east England (33, 68, 77, 112 and 113). Comprehensive regional control over all abstractions of water was established by the 1963 *Water Resources Act*, which set up the river authorities (Section 3) (119 p 3). In order to promote water conservation the *Act* laid down that

. . . no person shall abstract water from any source of supply in a river authority area, or cause or permit any other person to abstract any

water, except in pursuance of a licence under this Act granted by the
river authority . . . , (Section 23) (119 p 23).

There are, however, certain exceptions to this general restriction, one of
the most important being that no licence is required if the abstracted water
water is to be used for domestic or agricultural purposes other than spray
irrigation (Section 24 p 24). Any person who has abstracted water at any
time during the five years preceeding the *Act* is entitled to a licence of
right for the quantity of water abstracted. (Section 33 p 35.) New
abstractors have to apply for licences which are granted at the discretion
of the river authority, which bears in mind the availability of resources.
Each river authority is required by the *Act* to keep a register of all
licences issued and the public is allowed to inspect this record.

All the licences issued by the Kent, Sussex and Essex River Authorities
and by the Lee and Thames Conservancy Boards[9] were consulted, and the
quantity of water abstracted by each manufacturing concern was recorded.
Other information obtained from the registers was the exact location and
the nature of the source of the abstraction. In some cases it was also
possible to find out the type of manufacturing process, and the use to
which the water was put. No other statistical information about the
abstracting firms was available without taking a second survey, and so
regression analysis using the licence data was not feasible. The chief
method of analysis was, therefore, the mapping of each abstraction and
comparison of the resultant pattern of distribution with the distribution
of physical and human features in the 'study area'. (See Map 2.)
Information from the abstraction licences was also used to check the
accuracy of the replies to the 'Industrial Survey', and in addition it was
possible to find out some of the water using characteristics of those firms
which refused to answer or failed to respond to the questionnaire.

### 3 Metered supplies from water undertakings

Data on the quantity of water sold on a meter by some of the water
undertakings are available in *Water Statistics* (57) and in the *Water
Engineers' Handbook* (59), but these sources do not provide a complete
coverage for the whole study area. The information for the omitted areas
was obtained directly from the water undertakings themselves, which in
every case provided the requested data. Although metered water supplies
include some commercial and agricultural consumption, it was necessary
to use metered water figures as a proxy for industrial usage in the absence
of information for manufacturing units alone. Once again mapping was

the main method of analysis due to the difficulty of obtaining other data for areal units comparable with the supply areas of water undertakings. Employment exchange areas, and local government areas do not coincide with water undertaking areas and therefore the information obtained from each source cannot be statistically compared.

### The 'study area'

The 'study area' is not in fact one fixed area for all parts of the analysis since the information was not available for the same areal unit. There was, however, an attempt to make the areas coincide as nearly as possible. (See Map 1.) For the 'Industrial Survey' the sample frame was obtainable on a county basis, and it was therefore decided to study the counties of Essex, Hertfordshire, Buckinghamshire, Berkshire, Middlesex, London, Surrey, Sussex and Kent.[10] Information from the *Licence of Right Registers* was

**MAP 1   THE STUDY AREA**

available for river authority areas, although in some cases it was possible
to divide the areas into their component 'catchment zones'. The licences
were studied for the Essex, Lee, Thames, Sussex and Kent authorities,
which as Map 1 indicates, cover all the counties in the 'Industrial Survey'
As the Thames Conservancy Catchment Board area extends far outside
the south east, reaching into Gloucestershire, it was decided to omit any
of the 'catchment zones' that were further west than Reading. In the
analysis of metered water supplies, the water undertakings chosen for
study coincided as nearly as possible to the river authority areas.

No attempt was made to study the whole of the South Eastern region,
as defined by the *South-East Study* (126 p 1). The area to the north of
Essex and Hertfordshire was omitted as it is a distinct hydrological unit
based on the Great Ouse, rather than the Thames. It was also felt that
this northern zone was industrially distinct from the area to the south,
not having such strong economic ties with the London area. To the east
and south the boundary of the study area was fixed for convenience at
the coast. The western limit of the area was in fact the most difficult
to define, as no hydrological or administrative boundary could be used.
Finally, however, it was decided to omit the Hampshire and Dorset River
Authority areas and to omit that part of the Thames Conservancy
Catchment area that was west of Reading. These omissions were thought
advisable to keep the area of study down to manageable proportions.

# Chapter 2

# An economic evaluation of the water industry

**Introduction**
The first topic considered in this chapter will be the physical and
economic characteristics of water supply sources. In physical terms, water
is available in unlimited quantities as the sea represents a virtually
inexhaustible source of supply. There are, however, very real economic
limits to supply as resources have to be expended to collect, transport
and purify the water before it is ready for consumption. It is then
proposed to go on to discuss briefly the economic characteristics of the
different demands for water. This is necessary as the various uses of
water are highly interrelated; one pattern of consumption frequently
affects or even precludes some other possibility of development.
For example, the use of a river for navigation could be precluded, or at
least seriously hindered by the large-scale use of the same water course
for irrigation or industrial abstraction. As demand for the resource
increases, competition and conflict amongst the different users of both
surface and underground supplies are likely to become accentuated.
Industrial water use is just one of the competing demands for the limited
supplies of accessible and cheap water. Finally, in this chapter the
historical development and the legal framework of the water industry
will be looked at as these have affected the economic characteristics of
the industry and its efficiency as an instrument of resource allocation.

**Physical and economic characteristics of water supply**

1 *Physical and economic availability of water*
It is a frequently expressed opinion in the literature on British water
resources that in aggregate the country's precipitation represents a
quantity of water much greater than is ever likely to be required by the
community (94 p 5). Even allowing for the major and inevitable losses
through evapotranspiration the mean yield in England and Wales amounts
to about 40,800 million gallons per day (hereafter referred to as mgd) of
which only 4,653 mgd are currently utilized (94 p 5). To conclude from

such figures that the country has no water shortage problems is, however, erroneous. In the first place such statistics overestimate the recoverable supply of water, as it will never be physically possible to harness the whole amount of water even in areas used exclusively as gathering grounds. A large proportion is lost in soil moisture, and in too rapid return to the sea or the sewers. These losses through rapid run-off are greatly increased in urban areas (46 pp 347-51).

Mean yield figures also fail to take into account the very real distinction between physical availability and economically available resources. With a renewable and re-usable resource like water there is always more available to society at a price, and therefore there is no *physical* limit to supply and no *physical* shortage of water. Economic shortages arise, however, whenever the amount of water demanded is higher than that being supplied *at the going price.* If price is increased the quantity demanded will decrease and the quantity supplied will rise until equilibrium is regained and no shortage exists. At any one time an economic limitation on the expansion of water supplies will occur when the cost of obtaining extra quantities of the resource (the long-run marginal cost) rises above the value to society of the extra amounts obtained. In figure 1, an economic limit to supply ($Q1$) will occur where the demand curves ($DE_1$ and $DI_1$) and the long-run marginal cost curve ($LMC$) intersect. Only at this point is the cost of the last unit of water capacity equal to the value to society of that last unit. When demand increases ($DE_2$ and $DI_2$) the economic limit to supply will also be extended, the magnitude of the increase being partly determined by the elasticity of demand.[1]

If the demand for water is elastic ($DE$) a demand increase ($DE_1$ to $DE_2$) will result in a price increase to $P_2$ and an extension of the quantity taken to $Q_2$. On the other hand, the same shift in an inelastic demand curve will result in larger price ($P_3$) and quantity ($Q_3$) increases.

## 2 Spatial and temporal maldistribution of water supplies
Precipitation, and therefore the supply of water is maldistributed over space relative to the demand for the resource. Areas of relatively low precipitation coincide with not only the areas of highest evapotranspiration, but also with zones of high water demand. The south east area is the one chiefly affected by the maldistribution (93 p 11). Here a high density of population produces large demands from the industrial, commercial and domestic sectors, and it is also within this region that the scope for supplementary irrigation is highest. The problems caused by spatial maldistribution are magnified as the costs of overcoming distance

B*

**Figure 1 Economic limit on the expansion of developed water supplies**

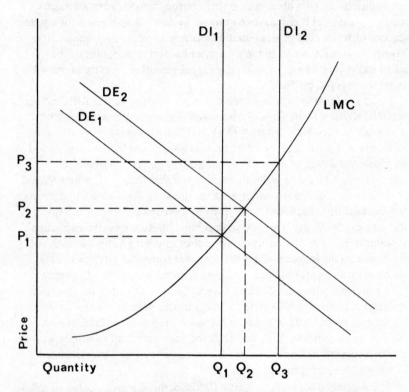

are exceptionally high due to the flow characteristics of water and to its bulky and low value nature. Therefore, water, unlike electric power, cannot economically be transported on a grid system, anything but short movement, or movement with gravity becomes prohibitively expensive (124 (c) p 13).

Not only does the supply of and demand for water suffer from spatial disequilibrium but there is also temporal maldistribution. In the first place, the total precipitation varies considerably from year to year, for example, Bilham has calculated that for the years 1863-1935 annual rainfall fluctuated within a range of 74% of the mean annual value (12 p 81). This implies that, unless the community is prepared to accept fluctuating levels of utilization, storage capacity must be provided to compensate for an abnormally low rainfall. Ideally, from the point of view of economic resource allocation, the amount of storage capacity constructed should reflect the consumers' willingness to pay for an assured supply. For example, it might be found that consumers are willing to pay an extra 6 pence per 1000 gallons to insure against a restriction of supply occurring every ten years, but that they were not prepared to pay an extra 1/- per 1000 gallons to guard against a twenty-five year shortage. In this case storage capacity should be below that needed to insure against a 1 in 25 year drought, but greater than that needed to counterbalance a 1 in 10 year deficit.

In addition to this annual variation in rainfall, seasonal fluctuations in the supply of, and the demand for, water also occur. On average, the distribution of rainfall is relatively uniform throughout the year, but water supplies vary considerably with fluctuations in evapotranspiration. As far as ground water supplies are concerned, rainfall occurring between May and September is largely irrelevant as little percolates to the water-table before being evaporated. Evaporation also greatly reduces the flow of surface water during the same months. Supply problems are caused by the coincidence of this period of lowest availability with the time of greatest demand. Both the domestic and agricultural sectors show a very pronounced summer peak in demand. The size of the peak tends to vary inversely with the available supplies, since any shortage of summer rainfall will not only decrease the supply of surface water but will also increase the demand for water for supplementary irrigation and garden watering. Industrial and commercial demands on the other hand are relatively stable throughout the year. Some manufacturers may well need proportionally more water for cooling due to the higher temperature and lower cooling capacity of the water, but this will be more than compensated for by the decrease in cooling water taken for electricity generation during the summer period (21 pp 44-5).

Whenever water suppliers have been faced with the problem of excess demand they have adopted two solutions. First, storage, transport and cleaning facilities have been developed irrespective of cost to meet all foreseeable peak demands in all areas. Secondly, administrative controls have been introduced on an *ad hoc* basis to curb demand at critical times or in critical areas. One of the most common forms of this control is the prohibition of garden watering during a drought. For historical and social reasons the water supply industry has neglected the possibility of solving the disequilibrium problems by price changes. The marginal cost of providing water at peak demand and low flow periods is very high; the construction of costly storage capacity is necessary and yet it will only be utilized for a few days each year. If peak price was set at the marginal

cost of this capacity price changes could be used to equate demand and
supply. As Figure 2 shows at peak demand the price of water and the
quantity provided is given by the intersection of *DP* with the long run and
short run marginal cost curves. During the off-peak period the water
industry will be operating within fixed capacity and, therefore, to use
a given scale of plant optimally, price and output should be set where the
off-peak demand curve (*DO*) cuts the short run marginal cost curve.

**Figure 2 Peak and off-peak water prices**

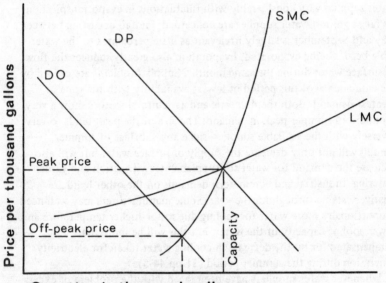

*DO* = Off-peak demand curve for water
*DP* = Peak demand curve for water
*LMC* = Long run marginal cost curve
*SMC* = Short run marginal cost curve

There are two distinct elements in the provision of additional summer
storage capacity: (a) Capacity is required to maintain a steady supply of
water over the year by supplementing low flow. (b) Storage is needed to
meet an increased demand for water. The cost of providing additional
facilities to counterbalance the summer decrease in supply should fall

equally on all consumers since they all benefit from the regular supply. On the other hand when extra capacity is needed to meet peak demands the cost should be met only by the section of the community imposing the demand.

### 3 *The cost curve for water*

Marginal cost pricing is the only system which maximizes *economic* efficiency in society; the marginal value to society of the water (as represented by price) is equal to the marginal opportunity cost.[2] There are, however, difficulties in the practical application of this pricing method to water supply. In the first place capital charges bear a high ratio to annual operating costs (40 p 222) and so only a proportion of the total cost of supply can be directly allocated to any particular unit of supply. Additionally, water capacity can only be built in large discrete lumps, which gives a *stepped marginal cost curve*. These two factors make it difficult to isolate the true marginal cost of supplying each unit of water.

It has been argued that once capacity has been constructed no opportunity costs are imposed on society by its use (78 pp 250-1), as the capital charges remain the same whether one gallon or one million gallons of water are taken. The use of the fixed capacity is optimized when price is set to equal the short-run marginal cost (which includes variable pumping and cleaning costs), but the short-run marginal cost curve lies below the long-run average cost curve, at least until demand nears or reaches the capacity of the equipment. This means that a deficit will be incurred during most of the life of the capacity, which may be as long as 100 years.

Other economists, on the other hand, have argued that indivisibilities[3] and the stepped marginal cost curve have made short-run marginal cost arbitrary (20 p 178). As Phelps-Brown and Wiseman say,

'Is it reasonable to say that no charge need be made as long as we are moving horizontally along one of the treads' . . . (of a stepped cost curve) . . . 'but that a charge springs up abruptly when we meet a riser' (20 p 180).

The authors go on to argue that long-run marginal cost pricing optimizes resource use in the long run, and that charges must include some interest and depreciation payments.[4] This type of pricing system would seem most appropriate in the water industry as it would overcome the problem of protracted deficits, which may have to be financed by borrowing.

**The economic characteristics of the different demands for water**
Traditionally the different demands for water have been left to develop
their resources independently on a local basis; this produced a fragmente(
and largely uncontrolled pattern of water use (124 (c) p 4). The
independent development has meant that wide differences occur in the
economic and organizational characteristics of the various sectional
interests in water. Although the *Water Resources Act*, 1963, has
established comprehensive regional control over all water uses in England
and Wales, this control has not yet had any significant impact on the
economic structure of each water use. It is therefore difficult to discuss
the economic characteristics of a water 'industry' as such, rather it is
proposed to briefly look at each sectional demand for water in turn. In all,
four groups of demands will be discussed, namely the water undertakings,
private abstractors, polluting bodies and amenity plus navigational
interests. More attention will be given to the first three groups as they all
concern manufacturing industry.

### 1 *Water supply undertakings*
Water undertakings influence industrial water supply in two distinct
ways: firstly they directly satisfy a sizeable proportion of industrial
demand,[5] and secondly they compete with private industrial abstractors
for the available supplies of cheap water. Their legal obligations, policies
and general efficiency therefore affect the availability and cost of water
used by manufacturers.

The primary legal obligation of statutory water undertakings in
England and Wales is to:

... provide in their mains and communication pipes a supply of
wholesome water sufficient for the domestic purposes of all occupiers of
premises. (1945 *Water Act*, Schedule 3, Section 31.)

Water undertakings are unable to refuse a supply to domestic consumers
living in areas where mains are laid, and also they have the duty to bring
water to any area where the aggregate amount of water rates payable
annually by householders in that area is 1/8th or more of the total expense
of providing and laying the pipes (1945 *Act*, Schedule 3, Section 29). In
addition, water must be provided on demand as no significant stockpiling
can occur, partly for health reasons, and partly due to the bulky nature of
water.

Only since the 1945 *Water Act* have the statutory suppliers been obliged to provide water for non-domestic uses. Section 27 of the *Act* laid down that:

Statutory water undertakers supplying water otherwise than in bulk shall give a supply of water on reasonable terms and conditions for purposes other than domestic purposes to the owner or occupier of any premises within their limits of supply who requests them to give such a supply to those premises. (p 29.)

Non-domestic consumers, however, still only have a limited right to a supply as it was laid down that domestic supplies take precedence in both quality and quantity. The undertakings are not required to provide an industrial supply,

. . . if their ability to meet existing obligations to supply water for any purposes or probable future requirements to supply water for domestic purposes, without having to incur unreasonable expenditure in constructing new waterworks for the purpose, would be endangered thereby. (Section 27, p 29.)

The availability of industrial supplies will depend on the amount of spare capacity held by any water undertaking, and on the willingness of local water engineers to expand their capital works to meet industrial demands. There is some evidence that a few water authorities are not prepared to extend their supply capacity even when industrial concerns are willing to pay the long-run marginal cost of their water (see chapter 6 p 156).

The bias in the water supply industry towards the domestic consumer is also illustrated by the fact that many water undertakings tend to regard themselves as a social service. As Bird and Jackson have pointed out,

The management structure of the water supply undertakings produces a built-in bias towards treating water supply as a social service. The great majority of their managers are engineers whose principal interest is sure to be in technical problems . . . Engineer managers are likely to prefer to look upon themselves as technological empire builders in a social service context. (14 pp 614-5.)

In part this social service view stems from the idea that water is a unique product, vital to life, and because of this it should be freely available to all irrespective of commercial considerations. It is also argued that water supply should be a social service linked to public health because some people would not or could not pay the full cost price of each unit of water used. However neither of these arguments are convincing. As Hirshleifer has pointed out, food and clothing are also vital to life and

yet we have adjusted to the idea that the purchaser must be prepared to
pay the going price to satisfy his wants (52 pp 4-5). To be consistent those
who advocate that water supply be treated as a social service ought also to
argue that all food, clothing and heat must be so supplied. As far as
the public health argument is concerned it is highly doubtful that many
people would refuse to pay for water which was required to maintain
health standards; today the needs of hygiene are well known. It is also
doubtful whether many people are unable to pay for water due to poverty,
and certainly the need to alleviate the poverty of a few is no argument for
providing low cost water to all domestic users.

Although there would appear to be no valid reasons for the water
undertakings supplying domestic consumers on a non-commercial basis,
the fact that a social service attitude has prevailed in the industry has
influenced the financial objectives of water undertakings, and it has
affected the methods used for charging domestic and industrial consumers.

The basic principle in the pricing policy of most water undertakings
is that over a period of years total annual revenue should equal total
annual cost; prices are set to achieve this result.[6] When estimating total
annual costs, the value of the variable costs (pumping, purification and
waste detection) are not difficult to calculate, but setting a value to annual
capital charges is more problematical. Most undertakings estimate their
annual fixed costs on the basis of historic cost (i.e. the actual past cost of
the installed capital equipment). This costing method is by no means
unique to water suppliers, but given their pricing policy it produces a
non-optimal allocation of resources. In many undertakings long-standing
equipment has been written off completely or at least much depreciated
in the accounts (15 pp 5-6). Interest charges on capital borrowed in the
past are likely to be well under those existing today, and in some cases
interest charges will no longer be recorded in the books of accounts as
the principal has been repaid. Capital charges calculated on the basis of
book past costs are therefore far below the cost of replacing the equipment
at present prices. Since fixed costs are normally a high proportion of total
costs, and as prices are set to recover the annual total costs, prices are
being set below the opportunity cost of water. Whilst supply capacity
is adequate to meet all demands the affects of underpricing are not felt,
but when demand increases can only be satisfied by new construction
then relatively large price increases are essential. As capacity is built on the
basis of a demand at deflated prices the undertakings may well be diverting
scarce resources away from uses more highly valued on the margin by
consumers. In addition the low cost of water is often used as a justification

of the present pricing methods, such circular reasoning results in the perpetuation of an inefficient resource allocation.

Although it has been said that prices are fixed to equate annual revenue and annual total cost, in fact most undertakings do not charge a *price* as such for water supplied to their domestic and commercial customers. In reality the consumer is charged for the provision of a water service as a flat rate is paid based on the rateable value of the property served. The unmetered domestic consumers do not pay a unit price for water, therefore, the resource can have no marginal value in use, and there is no incentive to economy. This feature is particularly important as supplies of water for present and probable future domestic consumption takes precedence over demands from manufacturers (116 p 29). Thus industrial growth may be limited in an area by the lack of suitable water supplies, whilst the householder is free to use as much as he likes, even to the extent of wasting it.

Industrial users are normally charged a price for each 1000 gallons of water taken; they receive a metered supply. Some undertakings also make a standing charge or meter rental in order to recoup a proportion of the fixed costs of supply. The standing charge is usually either based on the capacity of the supply pipes, or on the rateable value of the premises served. In some cases the addition of a standing charge to the quantity payment results in industrial consumers contributing twice to the undertakings fixed costs.

The main outlines of the pricing policy of water undertakings appear to be relatively consistent throughout the country; most authorities attempt to equate annual revenue with costs, and most differentiate between the unmetered domestic and the metered industrial consumer. When the charges are considered in more detail, however, it becomes apparent that there are considerable price variations, beyond those accounted for by cost differentials. In fact 'there is no uniformity in either the domestic charge, the trade charges, or the ratio of trade to domestic charge' (134 pp 137-8). Table 1 illustrates this point.

The average incomes obtained by undertakings from unmeasured and metered supplies are not directly comparable as unmeasured supplies include pipeline losses. It is, however, possible to make generous allowances for the level of wastage and then to compare the relative incomes. Undoubtedly in some undertakings industrial users directly subsidize the householder as the income per 1000 gallons of supply is greater from metered supplies than from unmetered water, after allowing for wastage.

**Table 1.** The average income derived by a selection of water undertakings from metered and unmeasured supplies, 1965-66

| Local Water Undertaking | Average income per 1000 gallons unmeasured supplies[7] 'd' | Average income per 1000 gallons measured supplies 'd' |
|---|---|---|
| Buckinghamshire Water Board | 32.51 | 47.83 |
| Chelmsford Borough | 38.48 | 52.74 |
| Colne Valley Water Company | 27.60 | 28.66 |
| Croydon Borough | 21.93 | 33.37 |
| Eastbourne Water Company | 32.69 | 30.25 |
| Medway Water Board | 22.67 | 30.84 |
| Metropolitan Water Board | 26.44 | 25.11 |
| Slough Borough | 13.51 | 26.63 |
| Thames Valley Water Board | 17.53 | 32.46 |
| Tunbridge Wells Borough | 46.55 | 46.72 |

Source: *Water Statistics.* Institute of Municipal Treasurers and Accountants. (57).

For example, if the Thames Valley Water Board charge equal amounts to industrial and household consumers for each 1000 gallons of water actually received, then pipeline losses would have to be approximately 2,700 million gallons per annum, which represents over 36% of the total annual supply. Similar levels of wastage would also have to occur in the Buckinghamshire, Chelmsford, Croydon and Slough Water Undertaking areas. In other undertakings industrial users subsidise the domestic consumer in a more indirect fashion; the subsidy only becomes evident when the relative costs of supplying the two groups are taken into consideration. Not only is the fixed cost of providing supply pipelines to one firm taking water in bulk less than that of supplying many household units, but, in addition industrial demand is relatively stable throughout the year and, therefore, the cost of providing capacity to supply a peak demand is not imposed. Subsidies tend to be large when undertakings, working under the third schedule of the 1945 *Water Act,*[8] require firms to pay a minimum annual charge based upon rateable value. It is in fact, becoming increasingly common, especially in the Metropolitan Water Board area, for manufacturing plants to have their meters removed as assessment on rateable value yields a higher revenue.

The cost burden is more evenly distributed between different types of consumer in some authorities, while in still others the domestic user subsidizes the industrialist. The latter case probably arises when a local authority wishes to attract industrial employment by providing cheap infrastructure services. One example of this did emerge in the 'Industrial Survey' (See chapter 5 page 128), but it is possibly more common in the development areas. This form of cross-subsidization is probably justified on the basis of expected returns, although normally, disturbance of the market allocative process results in inefficient resource allocation.

Both the costing methods and pricing policies of water undertakings are basic barriers to economic efficiency. As the water suppliers calculate their annual fixed costs on the basis of book past costs, the water they supply is typically underpriced, their capacity is overexpanded, and resources (water, construction equipment, land and labour) are being diverted away from uses valued more highly on the margin by consumers. This over-expansion of water undertakings supplies is important to the private industrial abstractor as they are in competition for the available supplies of cheap water for abstraction. The effect on the industrialist will probably be more marked in the future as the *Water Resources Act,* 1963, lays down that when river authorities issue abstraction licences they shall have particular regard to the duty of any relevant statutory water undertaking to provide supplies of water for domestic and public purposes (119 p 107).

Once the undertakings have developed their capacity they fail to allocate the available supplies between their customers in a way that maximizes economic efficiency. To maximize the welfare derived from any given quantity of water it should be allocated between consumers until its marginal value in use is equal for all consumers. While industrial users are required to pay a price for each unit of water used, the unmetered domestic consumer pays a fixed water rate unrelated to the quantity taken. This means that the marginal value in use of water supplied to a manufacturer is the price paid, whereas the domestic user takes water until the marginal value in use is zero. The transfer of some units of water from domestic to industrial consumers must result in a net increase of economic welfare.

## 2 *Private abstractors*

The term private abstractor refers to any concern, manufacturer or farmer, taking water directly from surface or underground sources. Private abstractors compete with each other and with the public water undertakings for suitable supplies of cheap water, and this competition cannot be optimally resolved by a market mechanism which produces equimarginal value in use. One reason for this is that water exhibits interdependencies in use, which results in a divergence between the private

and social costs of abstraction. Large tracts of land are hydrologically
interconnected, and therefore one persons' withdrawals will affect the
availability of water to all downstream users, or to all abstractors pumping
the same aquifer. The private cost of any withdrawal is the pumping and
piping costs, but the cost to society also includes the losses incurred by
the exclusion of an alternative use of water and the increased costs
imposed on all other users. Interdependencies in water also act as a
disincentive to conservation; no individual abstractor will attempt to
save water since any advantages will accrue equally to all other users of
the same aquifer or watercourse. A second reason why the free market
mechanism would produce a defective allocation of water for abstraction
is that it fails to take into account the degree of use to which a resource
is put. A price is paid for the quantity of water *used* and any positive
residual value of the resource after use would be ignored. For most
commodities this defect is of no consequence as the residual value is
zero, or negative, but as non-consumptive uses of water are common,
water is often left with a positive value. Therefore abstraction water is
not optimally allocated when equimarginal value *in use* is achieved, but
rather when each consumer is paying the full cost of his consumption
(or pollution) in terms of the foregone opportunities for other uses.
Price should therefore be set to equal marginal cost less the marginal
revenue earned on any residual water ($p = MC - [MR_a + MR_b$ to $MR_x]$).

In England and Wales the allocation of abstracted water is not left
to the free market mechanism but is allotted on a pro-rata or quota basis.
Abstractors established before 1963 were able to obtain a right to water
by paying a licence fee; concerns wishing to *begin* abstraction must first
get permission from the relevant river authority and pay the fixed licence
fee (119 p 23-44). In addition each abstractor pays an annual quantity
charge based on the gallonage which he is *entitled* to withdraw. Ideally
the price per 1000 gallons should reflect the degree of use to which the
water is put; in other words the price should reflect the opportunity cost.
The charging scheme recently published by the Thames Conservancy
Catchment Board does in fact approximate to this optimum pricing system;
irrigators pay a much higher rate than non-consumptive users, and
abstractors taking water solely during the summer period are charged a
peak price which is twice the normal all year round rate (114).

As yet the effectiveness of the licencing system cannot be judged as the
river authorities have not yet put the quantity charging schemes into
operation. There are, however, a number of factors which could lead to
an uneconomic allocation of water. In the first place all abstractors of the

same type within a river authority area pay the same price per 1000 gallons irrespective of the varying opportunity costs imposed. Some abstractors may be paying for water when the present opportunity cost is zero. A further difficulty will arise if in any water course the charges fail to remove excess demand. In this case an alternative allocative method will be required, and it would appear that the rationing criterion to be used by the river authorities is 'first come, first served' which will hardly produce the most economic distribution of water. Another feature which will probably result in a sub-optimal allocations is that domestic and agricultural users (other than spray irrigators) are not subject to the same licencing restrictions as are the other private abstractors (119 p 24). Although most domestic abstractors only withdraw water on a very small-scale, agricultural users may well markedly affect the local availability of water. There appears to be no logical reason why a factory producing bread should be charged for each 1000 gallons of water abstracted whereas a factory farm producing beef should be exempt. This feature will become of greater importance as intensive factory farming techniques become more widespread. A final factor which could lead to a non-optimal allocation of abstraction water is that water rights are to be assigned only to 'safe yield' or 'minimum acceptable flow' levels (119 pp 19-23); this immediately raises the problem of determining what constitutes a 'safe yield'. A more important defect with the whole concept is that it implies that water should not be *'mined'* (or that average annual abstraction should not exceed annual average replacement). An uneconomic allocation of the resource may occur as constant technology and prices are assumed.

### 3 Pollution interests

The use of a water course for trade effluent or sewage disposal may either exclude completely or at least raise the cost of subsequent uses; the degree of exclusion or cost increase will represent the opportunity cost to society of water used for dilution. To optimize the allocation of water between consumers the pollutor should pay this opportunity cost for water used.

In most cases the physical character of waste disposal is such that almost all the cost of pollution is external to the polluting unit. The private cost of pumping effluent into a stream is negligible for the discharger, but the social costs imposed may be high. This is then a classic case of technological external diseconomy, where the full marginal cost of water is not considered by the user. A distortion therefore appears in the optimum allocation of resources, and this may well have repercussions in other sectors of the economy. For example, if firm A pays a zero price for waste disposal, while imposing a cleansing cost of 1/- per 1000 gallons on a water using firm B, then the price of A's product will be underpriced with respect to B's; this will continue for firms using A's and B's products, and cumulative misallocation may result.

The problem is not to prevent all pollution, but to achieve the optimum allocation of water by imposing on the pollutor the true cost which is incurred. As Kneese points out:

A society that allows dischargers to neglect the offsite costs of waste disposal will not only devote too few resources to the treatment of waste, but will also produce too much waste in view of the damage it causes. (72 p 43).

In Britain the pollution problem has generally been misunderstood; attempts have been made to prohibit certain waste disposals but no attempt has ever been made to charge the pollutor for his use of water. To a certain extent prohibition is justified, for example, it is socially desirable to restrict the disposal of radioactive or poisonous materials, but this justifies only the selective prohibition of certain harmful pollutants and not that of all pollution. To date, the Acts which have been introduced to control effluent and sewage disposal have been relatively ineffectual (25 part II pp 1-6). Usually they have prohibited all new waste disposals while leaving untouched any discharger with prescriptive rights. This has tended to perpetuate past inefficient methods of waste disposal used by some firms while imposing too high disposal costs on others: cumulative distortion of the market system therefore may occur.

Most economists consider that a system of tax and bounty payments would be the most economically efficient method of tackling the pollution problem (72 pp 38-60). An alternative method of decreasing the amount of pollution would be to pay incentives to dischargers to clean the effluent before disposal. This method would, however, be economically inefficient as it merely subsidizes the disposal of effluent. With the tax and bounty scheme a public body would intervene to place on pollutors the full marginal cost of disposal. To quote Kneese once more:

in highly developed areas the offsite costs associated with unregulated waste discharge are likely to be great enough to justify public regulation, despite the costs and distortions which may be entailed in the regulation itself (72 p 54).

Although there are numerous problems involved in the calculation and apportioning of damages caused by pollution, undoubtedly a tax and compensation system would produce a more economically efficient allocation of water to effluent and sewage disposal. It is, however, possible that the level of pollution which is economically optimal will not be socially acceptable. If the demand for water for effluent and sewage disposal is inelastic (the elasticity of demand is as yet unknown), little improvement in the purity of rivers will occur and this may be regarded as socially undesirable. It should be clearly recognized, however, that any increase in river purity beyond the economic optimum will be costly to the economy.

### 4 *Amenity and navigation interests*

The use of streams and rivers for amenity and navigational purposes may well limit the availability of water for industrial use. If a stream is to be used for swimming, some control over pollution may be necessary, and, when a water course is made navigable, industrial and agricultural abstractions may have to be limited to maintain a minimum channel depth. As has been seen previously, competition between uses could be resolved by charging the marginal opportunity cost of the water required. Considerable difficulties arise, however, in the determination of the marginal cost of navigation and recreation uses because of indivisibilities; for example the cost of maintaining a navigable waterway would be the same whether one vessel or many used the channel. It is also difficult to express in money terms the benefits which people derive from amenity and recreational uses of water. In the past, these benefits were regarded as intrinsically intangible, but increasingly attempts are being made to evaluate them by estimating the price people *would* be willing to pay to enjoy the facilities (55, 22, 111). Despite the difficulties involved in determining marginal costs and benefits it is important that some attempts to calculate them are made, because in their absence there is a danger of either under- or over-estimating the value of recreation and amenity when allocating water between competing uses. For example, it is common to hear such statements as a loss of '190 tons of salmon and grilse with an ex-river value at present day prices of some £160,000' is caused each year by river pollution in the rivers Tyne and Tees (9 p 60), but the figure mentioned does not represent the true loss (cost) to society of pollution. The real social costs involved are the loss of the fish *plus* the loss of benefit derived from recreational fishing *less* the gains from the transfer of the resources used in fishing, including the water, to alternative uses.

**The legal and historical background as an explanation of the present
economic characteristics of the water industry**
 A major feature in the development of the water industry has been the
lack of attention paid to water planning on a national basis. Throughout
the nineteenth century the laissez-faire climate restricted any extension
of central control over water supply, and in fact such control was largely
unnecessary as water supplies were adequate to meet the relatively small
and localized demands.(123 p 46). The piecemeal unregulated development
of the industry has, however, influenced the present day economic
characteristics and the structure of the various demands for water.
Resources have not been exploited in such a way as to make possible
the supplying of all the various demands from the most economic sources.
For example, there are many small water undertakings and private
abstractors who have developed supplies to meet small specific
requirements without fully utilizing site capacity; this feature is important
as the enlarging of capacity once construction has occurred is often
difficult and costly (94 p 6). Over the years, the numerous abstractors
(private and public) and *in situ* users have produced a competitive and
economically inefficient system of water supply. The *Water Acts* of
1945 and 1963 have been introduced to rectify the situation by providing
a unified mangement of water for all uses.
   In the past, the only governmental controls over water supplies were
designed to safeguard public health, and this interest in health has greatly
influenced the economic characteristics of certain sectors of demand.
During the eighteenth and nineteenth centuries industrial and urban
development caused a rapid deterioration in the purity of the rivers.
By 1850 it became apparent that the situation whereby a riparian owner
was entitled to discharge effluent or sewage into a water course was
untenable, especially as pollutors who had established a prescriptive right
to discharge into a river could not be legally challenged; the argument
that the sewage or trade effluent was damaging downstream water users
had no relevance in law (137). From 1847 to 1951 a series of largely
ineffectual Acts and Commissions attempted to control river pollution (74).
Most of the Acts contained a straight prohibition of all new effluent or
sewage discharges, without any attempt being made to calculate the
benefits and costs of the control, and without providing alternative means
of disposal. There were three main reasons why the Acts failed to make
any material improvement in river purity. In the first place established
pollutors were normally left uncontrolled. Secondly, there was a general
reluctance to impose fines and other sanctions on concerns ignoring the

provisions of the Acts. Finally, it was usual for the local sewage authorities
to be responsible for enforcing the Acts and they themselves were amongst
the worst offenders. The effects of this lack of effective control are
still being coped with today by the machinery established by the 1951
and 1961 *Rivers Acts,* but even the latest legislation fails to identify the
true problem with water pollution, which is to place the costs of waste
disposal on the discharger.

The influence of the government's interest in health and hygiene is
very noticeable in the present costing and pricing policies of water
undertakings. Charging domestic consumers on rateable value is a relic
of the time when people had to be encouraged to use sufficient water
to increase the standards of public health. Similarly the health interest
can be seen in the bias towards the domestic consumer which occurs in
the 1945 *Water Act* (116 p 29), and which often exists in the charging
schedules of statutory water undertakings.

The historical development of the water industry has affected
manufacturers in three major ways. Firstly, the piecemeal unregulated
growth of water supply has meant that demands are sometimes not met
from the most economic sources of supply; costs of private abstraction
and the prices paid for water from the statutory undertakings may well
have been increased. Secondly, the lack of effective control over river
pollution has increased costs for some private abstractors requiring a good
quality water supply, whilst subsidizing the disposal of trade effluents;
this results in a misallocation of resources, including water, between
consumers. Finally the traditional linkage of the water supply industry
with public health has meant that domestic consumers take precedence
over industrial users, both in the availability and security of supply, and
often in the price they pay.

**Conclusions**
In some parts of Britain, especially in the summer months, the quantity
of water desired exceeds the available supplies. This disequilibrium will
become more marked in the future unless the supply of water is increased
or the quantity taken is reduced. Such disequilibria exist in virtually every
commodity used by man; water is in no way unique in this respect. In
Britain, however, the method used to regain an equilibrium position in
water supplies is not the one commonly used to reduce shortages of other
goods. Until recently no attempt was made to reduce the quantity of
water taken, but supply increases were made regardless of cost until no
shortages existed. Even today future levels of water consumption are

calculated by extrapolating past trends (with some adjustments for population change, industrial growth, and the expansion of irrigation) and then capacity is constructed to meet the 'requirements'. For example, the Water Resources Board's Technical Committee on water supplies in south east England have calculated that by the year 2001, a deficiency of 1,100 mgd will probably exist, which will require an expenditure of between £710 and £850 millions to extend supplies (127 pp 5-13). Not only are the possible effects of recent legislation ignored, but also the possibility of rationing water by changing its price is not considered. The assumption is made that once 'requirements' have been calculated, the only remaining problem is to find new sources of supply.

It would be impossible to rectify shortages of all goods by increasing the supply as the economy's resources are not indefinitely expandable. There appear to be no rational grounds for allowing water supplies to be extended to meet all foreseeable 'needs', when the supply of most other commodities is only increased when the consumers are prepared to pay for the increase by foregoing alternative goods. It is possible that the construction of additional water supply capacity is diverting resources away from uses valued more highly on the margin by consumers.

Once a given capacity has been developed the water industry does not allocate the available supplies optimally between consumers. It is suggested that too many resources are being used to supply the domestic sector. As householders do not pay a unit price for their water, there is no marginal value in use and there is no incentive to save water. This feature is particularly important since present and future domestic requirements are given precedence over industrial supplies. In addition too many resources are probably being devoted to effluent and sewage disposal as pollutors are not charged the opportunity cost of the water they use. Although the licencing of abstractions may well provide a good basis for the economic reorganization of the water industry it would appear that agricultural abstractors (other than spray irrigators) will be exempt from licencing controls and will not have to pay for abstracted water. This could result in a diversion of water into agricultural uses when it could be used more profitably in industry (140).

# Chapter 3

# The present patterns of industrial water use

In recent years the government has become more involved in water resource planning and conservation; it is therefore important to know the likely reaction of water users to planning regulations. For example, there are three possible ways in which abstractors may react to the provisions of the 1963 *Water Resources Act*. There could be an increase in the total quantity of water withdrawn from private sources due to the greater security of abstraction by right. Alternatively, the gallonage charge may decrease private abstraction and shift the demand for water to the statutory undertakers. Or finally it is possible that a net decrease in water consumption may occur with the introduction of water saving equipment. The probable reaction of water users to planning controls can only be known with any degree of certainty when the variables affecting the level of water consumption have been isolated and understood. Reliable forecasts of the quantity of water required in the future also need an understanding of the functional relationships that exist between the demand determinants and the level of water consumption.

In this chapter an attempt will be made to isolate the factors underlying the consumption of water by one sector of the market for the resource, namely manufacturing industry. In this attempt the uses for which industry takes water will first be considered, as these affect not only the quantity and quality of water that is required but also the sources from which the demand is satisfied. The spatial pattern of industrial water usage in south east England will then be analysed, and areal variations in the intensity of use picked out, from which it may be possible to deduce some of the factors underlying the distribution. Finally, as the spatial (or total) usage patterns are created by agglomerations of single water-using manufacturing units the determinants of the variation in the quantity of water taken by individual firms will then be considered. In the following chapter the analysis will be continued by subdividing the firms responding to the 'Industrial Survey' into industry type groups, and discussing the causes of inter- and intra-industry differences in demands.

## The uses of water in manufacturing industry

The most common use of water in manufacturing plants is staff hygiene
and welfare; only five firms out of the 253 respondents to the 'Industrial
Survey' claimed not to use water for this purpose. On average the sample
firms take just over 11 gallons of water per employee per day for staff
hygiene. This figure is within the range of 10 to 15 gallons per employee
per day mentioned by Hopthrow as being the average for British industry
(54 p 30). Improving standards of employment are, however, causing a
steady increase in the average consumption per employee. Although
sanitation is an important use it accounts for only approximately 8% of
the total water taken by the sample firms. This percentage, however, is
subject to error as some of the respondents were unable to distinguish
between the quantity of water used for hygiene and that used in the
manufacturing processes. The figure of 8% is well below the 26%
mentioned in the United Nations' publication *Water for Industrial Use*
as the average for firms in the United States (128 p 4). In part the
divergence between the two percentages may reflect higher standards
of employment and a greater use of air conditioning equipment in the
United States. It is, however, probable that the difference between the
two countries is more apparent than real, being the result of different
methods of calculating the percentages. The 8% figure was reached by
totalling the amount of water used for all purposes by the respondent
firms, and then calculating the amount used for sanitation as a percentage
of this. On the other hand it is thought that the American percentage was
found by taking the average (mean, median or modal) percentage used
for sanitation and welfare by individual firms. A simple numerical
example will illustrate this point. Firm A takes 10 million gallons per year
(mgy), all of which is used for staff purposes. Firm B takes 100 mgy but
uses only 10% of this for sanitation. The total water used by the firms
equals 110 mgy, of which only 20 mgy or 18% is used by the employees.
On the other hand the average percentage of water used for this purpose
in the two firms is 55% ([100% + 10%]/2).

In terms of the quantity of water taken cooling far exceeds all other
water uses, being responsible for between 65% and 70% of all water used
by the sample firms. This figure has important implications for water
conservation since most cooling water is returned to the stream course
with little diminution in quantity or quality (except for some increase in
temperature): an opportunity to re-use therefore exists. In this country,
water is still the most economical agent for the rapid dissipation of excess
heat (54 p 31), and it was used for this purpose by 61% of the respondent

firms. The scale of usage varies greatly, however, being highest in power generation, chemical manufacture, oil refining and paper making.

A third common use of water by manufacturers is to produce steam for use in mechanical processes, such as power generation, or in chemical and physico-chemical operations, such as distillation. Although 74% of the respondents took water for steam raising, the actual quantity of water involved is small, representing only approximately 4% of the total water taken. However, the quality requirements for water used to produce steam are often stringent (54 p 31). For example, the dissolved solids and silica content must be low to reduce scaling and corrosion in pipes and boilers; extensive pre-use treatment of the water is therefore common.

A further 14% of the total water used is employed in the actual manufacturing processes, which include incorporation into the product, dissolving and diluting soluble substances, and scrubbing industrial gases to remove pollutants. For many of these process purposes the manufacturers require a high quality water supply, although potability is not necessary unless the water is incorporated into an edible product. In all, 72% of firms used a proportion of their supply in manufacturing processes.

There are only three other uses which involve important gallonages of water. Firstly, it is used to wash down plant and materials, secondly, for conveying substances in solution or suspension, and thirdly for fire fighting. The latter use rarely involves large scale water consumption, but supplies must be constantly available at adequate pressures.

In addition to uses which involve the actual removal of water from streams or aquifers, industry also uses water *in situ*, especially for effluent dilution. 22% of the respondents disposed of part or all their effluent directly into water courses, while the remainder use them indirectly via the local sewage system. Other *in situ* uses include the transportation of bulky, low value raw materials and occasionally the generation of power. The latter use is of negligible importance at the present time but some abstraction licenses of right have been claimed for this purpose (68), which may require the total flow of a stream thus precluding consumptive upstream uses.

### Sources of industrial water supply

In the past manufacturing industries were expected to obtain their water requirements by private abstraction, either from surface sources or underground strata. Although some local water undertakings were selling supplies to industrialists as early as 1850 (110 p 14), they had no general duty to do so and usually only undertook to provide a supply if they had a surplus over domestic requirements. The situation has changed so much today that virtually all firms rely on the statutory water undertakings for at least part of their requirements. From the returns of the 'Industrial Survey' it would appear that only 1.8% (i.e. five firms) of firms in the south east rely solely on their own abstracted supplies. Water is not a homogeneous good; each water quality is to some extent a separate product for which other qualities are not perfect substitutes. Manufacturers must provide a potable supply of water for their employees but the same quality is rarely needed in the actual production processes unless water enters or comes into contact with a consumable product, such as in food, drink and pharmaceutical manufacture. However, such uses account for a very small proportion (less than 1%) of total industrial water consumption. It is wasteful to use bought water for purposes not requiring this standard as the price incorporates an element for treatment up to potability. For this reason manufacturers with access to private sources of supply tend to reserve purchased water for staff hygiene purposes while privately abstracting water to satisfy their demands for other qualities. Any treatment of privately abstracted supplies can produce the required quality without incurring any wasteful expense by over cleaning.

Where manufacturers cannot abstract enough water to meet all their requirements, it is possible that they would consider purchasing a non-potable supply from local water undertakings. Such a supply is already provided by a few statutory undertakings, for example Neath Rural District, St Helens County Borough and the West Hampshire Water Company (57). It would be necessary for individual authorities to test the economic feasibility of providing this type of supply. From the survey results it appears that 35% of firms would consider taking a low priced non-potable supply, and it is possible that this percentage would increase when the effects of the 1963 *Water Resources Act* are felt.

Although most firms purchased some water, in absolute quantity terms private abstraction is the most important source of supply. In general the price of bought water precludes its use when very large quantities are required. The respondent firms paid on average only 1.33 pence per 1,000 gallons[1] for their abstracted supplies, whereas 48.1 pence[2] was the average price of 1,000 gallons of purchased water. This latter figure did decrease, however, to 34.4 pence when only firms supplied on a meter were included.

Purchased supplies of water accounted for only 10.3% of the total water used by respondent firms. As the composition of firms replying

to the 'Industrial Survey' does not conform to the composition of
manufacturing industry in the south east, it was necessary to weight the
percentage figures to obtain a value for the proportion of purchased
supplies in the total water taken by manufacturers in the south east.
The new weighted percentage was 12.9%, which is significantly below
a value of 21% which can be derived from the industrial consumption
figures quoted in the *First Report* of the Sub-Committee on the Growing
Demand for Water (149 (a) p 28). The Sub-Committee stated that in 1955,
38% of total public supply was sold by meter to industry, and that
industry abstracted privately an amount equal to the total public supply.[3]
These figures imply that 21% of total industrial supply is purchased from
statutory water undertakings.

There would appear to be four possible reasons for the discrepancy
between the two percentages. Firstly, it is possible that the 'Industrial
Survey' underestimates the proportion of water purchased by being
biased towards firms withdrawing water from private supply sources.
Initially it was thought that such a bias could have resulted from private
abstractors being more prepared to answer a questionnaire on industrial
water use, especially as the new licencing requirements would have brought
the subject to the management's attention. It was possible to test this
hypothesis by checking the registers of abstractors to see whether the
respondents included a larger proportion of abstractors than did
the non-respondents. 17.2% of the respondents owned their own sources
of supply whereas 23.4% of the non-respondents had applied for licences
of right. Therefore it is unlikely that private abstractors are
over-represented in the 'Industrial Survey'.

The Sub-Committee on the Growing Demand for Water referred to
industrial consumption in the whole of England and Wales. It is therefore,
possible that the 'study area' contains proportionately more industries
abstracting large quantities of water than the country as a whole and
that this is the reason for the discrepancy between the two percentages.
Intuitively, it is not thought that this explanation is a likely one as the
south east contains proportionately less heavy industry than many other
regions. However an analysis of the abstraction licences granted by river
authorities outside the 'study area' would be necessary before an accurate
judgement could be made.

It is also possible that the rate of expansion of abstracted supplies
has been greater than that of purchased supplies since the sub-committee's
estimates were made in 1955. In recent years there has been a rapid
expansion of large water-using industry, such as oil refining and plastics

manufacture, and these do satisfy much of their demand for water by private abstraction. But it is unlikely that differential rates of growth between abstracted and purchased supplies would be great enough to explain the whole discrepancy between the percentages.

A final possibility is that the sub-committee has underestimated the quantity of water privately abstracted by industry. As no licence of right registers were available in 1955 such an under-valuation seems likely and is easily understandable.

The respondent firms obtained over 72% of the water which they abstracted privately from surface sources of supply. This high percentage is primarily the result of a few very large abstractions of over 100 million gallons per annum. An analysis of the licences of right for south east England confirmed that only approximately 30% of privately abstracted water was obtained from underground sources, but this appears to contradict the opinion of Dr D. H. Sharp, Technical Director of the Federation of British Industry who has stated that,

probably the greatest source of these abstractions is from private wells and bore holes but, in addition, considerable quantities are drawn direct from rivers and streams (100 pp 59-60).

From the abstraction licences and the test interviews it was found that water from rivers, canals and tidal estuaries is usually used for cooling, whereas ground water is more commonly used in the actual manufacturing process.[4] The quality requirements of cooling water are not usually stringent although the level of biological slimes, weeds and animal life must be controlled as they affect the rate of heat transfer and may block the cooling system (54 p 31). Water quality is usually a more vital consideration when it is used in the actual manufacturing process, and so for these purposes ground water is preferred to surface supplies.

**Spatial water usage patterns**
Industrial demands for water from both water undertakings and private abstraction have produced a distinct spatial pattern of water usage in south east England. These demands were mapped in the hope that areal variations in use would emerge, from which it would be possible to isolate some of the factors underlying the spatial distribution. Statistical analysis of the data was not attempted as the information was not available for comparable areal units.[5]

As collected statistics of total industrial water use are not available it was necessary to examine separately the usage patterns for water

abstracted privately by manufacturers, and for water purchased by
them from local water undertakings. Information on abstracted water
was obtained from the licence of right registers kept by the Kent (68),
Sussex (112) and Essex (33) River Authorities, and by the Thames (113)
and Lee (77) Conservancy Catchment Boards. Published figures of metered
water supplied by each water undertaking in the 'study area' have been
used as a surrogate for the quantity of water purchased by manufacturers
(57 and 59). It is, however, recognised that these are by no means an ideal
measure as many undertakings also meter commercial and agricultural
premises, which fall outside the scope of this enquiry. As some authorities
do not make any distinction in their records between industrial and
commercial users, it has proved impossible to avoid the use of unrefined
metered figures. No spatial information has been derived from the
'Industrial Survey', since this was stratified into industry groups, and
designed to give statistically reliable results for industry as a whole and
for functional sub-groups. Although the survey did obtain responses
from firms scattered throughout the 'study area', there is no guarantee
that the results would be reliable for spatial sub-units. No attempt was
made to devise a sample frame stratified into both industry and spatial
groups as this would have greatly increased the size of the sample needed.
It was thought that industry group stratification was more vital as space is
usually not a primary but a derived variable in explaining water usage.[6]

## 1 *Abstracted supplies*

Each industrial abstraction, for which a licence of right has been claimed,
was plotted over a base map showing the physical and urban characteristics
of the 'study area' (see map 2). Most manufacturing units currently
abstracting either surface or ground water are included, although any new
withdrawals for which a manufacturer is not entitled to a licence of right
will not be recorded.

The most noticeable element in the spatial distribution is the
concentration of private abstractions occurring along the River Thames,
and its tributaries, most notably the Wye (Buckinghamshire), the Colne,
Lea, Darenth and Medway. This is not, however, to suggest that all the
withdrawals of water in these belts are from surface sources. It is common
for an industrialist to use ground water in his manufacturing processes,
while taking surface water for cooling. For example, the Shell oil refinery
at Shellhaven (33), withdraws over 42,000 million gallons per annum
from the tidal Thames, plus a further 82 million gallons per annum from
the chalk. Likewise the Wiggins Teape group is licensed to abstract

c

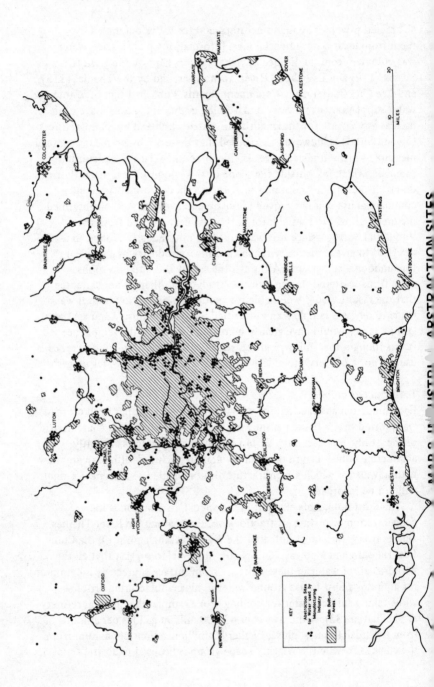

MAP 3 INDUSTRIAL ABSTRACTION SITES

2235 million gallons from the River Darenth and a further 1101.5 million gallons by bore (68). Linked with the riverside clustering is the second element in the spatial pattern, which is that the largest concentrations of abstractors are conspicuous by their proximity to London.

Watercourses have long been foci for urban and industrial development and the drained marshlands along lower Thameside, from the Tower of London to the Isle of Grain, have attracted a wide variety of manufacturing units. Four industry groups dominate the industrial structure of the area: cement, paper, public utilities and the processing of imported raw materials (28 pp 64-6). All of these types of manufacture involve the use of large quantities of water in process, for cooling, and in the case of cement producers for the conveyance of slurry. The agglomeration of these types of industry is a major factor causing the clustering of abstraction points along lower Thameside. Many of the abstractions are very large, often over 100 mgy, and so the concentration of abstraction within this area is even more marked when the actual quantities involved are considered. East of Gravesend there is a noticeable falling off in the number of abstraction points, which reflects the decreasing attractiveness of the riverside as distance from London increases.

The concentration of major water-using industry in north Kent is also an important factor behind the cluster of abstraction sites along the rivers Darenth and Medway. In fact the Darenth acts as a small extension of lower Thameside and has a very similar industrial structure. Paper and board manufacturing is by far the most important industry in the pattern of water withdrawals in north Kent; it accounts for a quantity of water far exceeding that taken by any other industry group (see table 2). Other industries which demand large gallonages of water include cement manufacture and the processing of imported raw materials, such as leather. Most of the remaining abstractors in the area are oriented towards local urban markets; for example Fremlin Pale Ale Limited have applied to take 12 million gallons a year from bores at Maidstone, and Blue Cap Foods require 34.8 mgy for cooling and 8.7 million for processing at their Ditton factory (68).

A third cluster of abstractions occurs in the Lea Valley and neighbouring parts of east London. The growth of manufacturing to the west of the Lea in the Hackney–Stoke Newington area was closely linked with the early 19th Century spread of residential building into the Lea Valley (139 p 45). Concentrations of labour or market-oriented industry almost inevitably include a proportion of firms requiring process or cooling water. It would seem likely that such firms abstracted from boreholes or located to the

**Table 2.** Abstractions made by industrialists in the Darenth and Medway valleys

| Industry Group | Quantity Taken (in mgy) | Percentage of Total |
|---|---|---|
| Paper | 13239.2 | 86.8% |
| Drink | 619.3 | 4.0% |
| Food | 47.5 | 0.3% |
| Textiles & Leather | 28.8 | 0.2% |
| Rubber & Plastics | 96.0 | 0.6% |
| Chemicals | 200.7 | 1.3% |
| Non-Metallic Minerals | 651.9 | 4.2% |
| Engineering | 152.0 | 0.9% |
| Other | 221.2 | 1.4% |

Data for this table was obtained from the Kent River Authority's Abstraction
*Register* (68).

nearest available surface source, whenever the local water undertaking
would not provide a supply for industry, or when the quantity required
exceeded that which could be economically purchased. The chief market-
oriented abstractors in the Lea area are drink manufacturers, scattered
throughout east London, confectioners in the Wood Green area, and a
biscuit manufacturer. Many primary processing firms or public utilities
have also been attracted to the Lea by the ease of importing raw materials,
such as coal, timber, non-ferrous metals, sugar and chemicals. These firms
commonly demand large quantities of water both for processing and
cooling. Public utilities are exceptionally large abstractors from the
lower Lea, for example, the Central Electricity Generating Board is
licensed to take 53,268 mgy from the navigation and the Lea downstream
from Brimsdown, and the North Thames Gas Board is licensed to abstract
331 mgy downstream from Leyton. Other large abstractors, taking over
50 mgy include Enfield Rolling Mills, Ruberoid Ltd., and British Feeding
Mills Ltd. (77). To the north of Enfield the majority of abstractors are
working sand and gravel; in such cases the abstraction is usually designed
to pump excess water from the workings rather than to use the water for
processing or cooling.

Market- or labour-oriented industry account for the majority of the
abstractions to the west of London, along the Wye, Thames and Colne
Valleys. Industrial development began on a large scale towards the end
of the 19th Century, and has been associated primarily with proximity
to the London market and with the major transport routes through the
area to the West Midlands and to Bristol. Development of this kind

virtually inevitably includes a proportion of firms which require water
in quantities exceeding those which can be purchased economically.
Most of these firms are in the food, drink and chemical industries, although
occasionally firms producing plastics, textiles and engineering products
will abstract water privately.

The pattern of abstractions to the west of London has also been
influenced by the concentration of three large water-using industries in
parts of the area; these are non-metallic minerals, paper making and
furniture manufacture. A considerable number of abstractors in the
Thames flood plain and along the Taplow terrace are working sand and
gravel; most of the pumping takes place to remove excess water from the
workings. Paper manufacturers cluster around two centres in the area, the
Wye valley near High Wycombe, and the Upper Colne near Hemel
Hempstead. Furniture manufacturers are also concentrated around High
Wycombe. In terms of the quantity of water taken paper makers are by
far the most important abstractors, and water availability was one factor
in the location of the industry along the Wye. As Embleton and Mountjoy
have said;

The industry needed a water supply for providing power and making pulp
from rags, mainly obtained from old clothes. The Wye water was found to
be free from iron salts and other impurities that might stain paper. (32 p 92).

From the mapping of private abstraction points it would appear that the
density of abstractors and the quantity of water taken in any area is closely
related to the degree of industrial concentration and to the type of industry
present. Most urban areas have attracted some firms that find it economic
to obtain water privately, but the greatest quantities of water are
abstracted in areas where primary processing firms and public utilities
are agglomerated. It was found that physical factors have played an
essentially passive role in the determination of the pattern of industrial
water usage. Within the framework set by the availability of abstraction
sources firms tend to locate to those pumping sites that are nearest to the
urban centres. Only rarely has water acted as a positive factor in the
location of industry within an area, although it is possible that as more
potentially suitable sites are tapped the physical availability of water will
become a more important location factor. It was, however, found from
direct enquiries to industrialists that any contraction in available
abstraction sites is being offest by technical developments in water-saving
equipment and by the substitution of purchased metered supplies. The
locational importance of water will be considered in detail in Chapter 5.

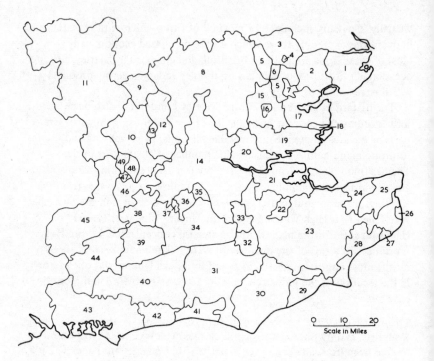

## MAP 3  THE STATUTORY WATER UNDERTAKINGS, 1966

Key to map 3

**Statutory water undertakings, 1966**

 1 Tendring Hundred Water Works
   Company
 2 Colchester and District Water
   Board
 3 Halstead Rural District Council
 4 Halstead Urban District Council
 5 Braintree Rural District Council
 6 Braintree and Bocking UDC
 7 Witham Urban District Council
 8 Lee Valley Water Company
 9 Luton Water Company
10 Rickmansworth and Uxbridge
   Valley Water Co.

11 Buckinghamshire Water
   Company
12 Colne Valley Water Company
13 Watford Borough Council
14 Metropolitan Water Board
15 Chelmsford Rural District
   Council
16 Chelmsford Urban District
   Council
17 Maldon Rural District and
   Borough Council
18 Burnham-on-Crouch Urban
   District Council

19 Southend Water Works Company
20 South Essex Water Works Company
21 Medway Water Board
22 Maidstone Water Works Company
23 Mid-Kent Water Company
24 Canterbury and District Water Company
25 Thanet Water Board
26 Deal Borough Council
27 Dover Borough Council
28 Folkestone and District Water Company
29 Hastings County Borough Council
30 Eastbourne Water Works Company
31 Mid-Sussex Water Company
32 Tunbridge Wells Borough Council
33 Sevenoaks and Tonbridge Water Company
34 East Surrey Water Company
35 Croydon London Borough Council
36 Sutton District Water Company
37 Epsom and Ewell Borough Council
38 Woking and District Water Board
39 Guildford, Godalming and District Water Board
40 North West Sussex Water Board
41 Brighton County Borough Council
42 Worthing Borough Council
43 Portsmouth Water Company
44 Wey Valley Water Company
45 Mid-Wessex Water Company
46 South West Suburban Water Company
47 New Windsor Borough Council
48 Slough Borough Council
49 Burnham, Dorney and Hitcham Water Works Company

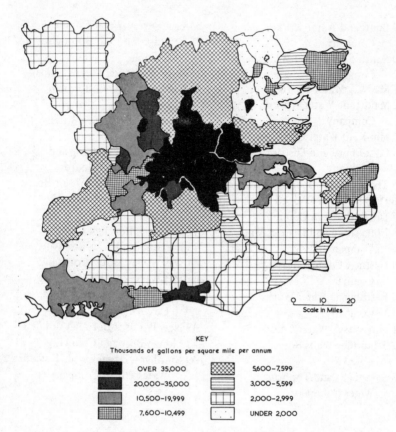

KEY

Thousands of gallons per square mile per annum

| | | |
|---|---|---|
| ■ | OVER 35,000 | 5,600–7,599 |
| | 20,000–35,000 | 3,000–5,599 |
| | 10,500–19,999 | 2,000–2,999 |
| | 7,600–10,499 | UNDER 2,000 |

## MAP 4   METERED WATER SUPPLIED PER SQUARE MILE BY THE STATUTORY WATER UNDERTAKINGS

*2 Industrial water supplies purchased from water undertakings*
Three octile maps have been constructed using data on metered water
supplied by the statutory water undertakings within the study area.
These maps show metered water use per square mile, metered water use
per person resident in the undertaking's area and finally metered water
as a percentage of the total water supplied (pp 42-5). From the maps it
would appear that the spatial pattern of metered water use is influenced
by three interrelated factors; firstly the density of manufacturing
employment, secondly the relative position of manufacturing in the

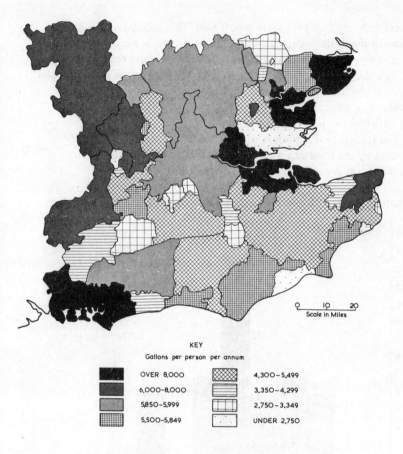

KEY

Gallons per person per annum

| | |
|---|---|
| OVER 8,000 | 4,300–5,499 |
| 6,000–8,000 | 3,350–4,299 |
| 5,850–5,999 | 2,750–3,349 |
| 5,500–5,849 | UNDER 2,750 |

## MAP 5   METERED WATER SUPPLIED PER RESIDENT BY STATUTORY UNDERTAKINGS

total employment structure of an area, and finally the type of industry present.

Clearly there is a relationship between the level of urban development (and therefore the density of manufacturing employment) and the quantity of metered water purchased. This arises because market and labour oriented industries must provide a potable supply of water for staff hygiene purposes. Most of the urban areas stand out with high metered water use per square mile and per resident (maps 4 and 5). Metered water usage per square mile is highest within the Metropolitan Water Board area,

c*

where some 68 mgy per square mile is sold. This gallonage probably
underestimates the industrial consumption as there is a growing practice
of removing meters and charging manufacturers a water rate based on
the rateable value of the factory. Although the quantity of metered water
taken in an area is partially determined by the number of persons
employed the relationship is by no means a perfect one since many
industries do use purchased water in process.

The frequency distribution of the gallonage of water supplied per
resident by the statutory water undertakings is significantly different
from one which could have arisen randomly (figure 3).

**Figure 3 The quantity of metered water supplied per resident per annum**

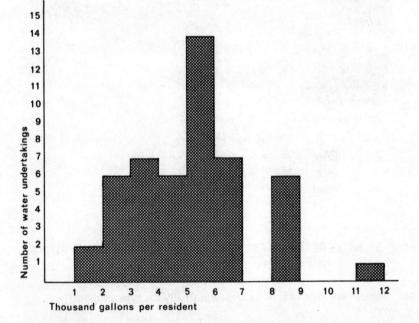

Over 50% of the undertakings in the study area supplied between 4,100
and 6,100 gallons per annum per resident. It is suggested that this
noticeable mode results from the fact that the quantity of water needed
per employee for staff hygiene purposes within factories does not vary
greatly. The range of values in the distribution probably is produced by
two factors, firstly some firms use metered water in process, and secondly,
the proportion of residents employed locally varies between undertaking

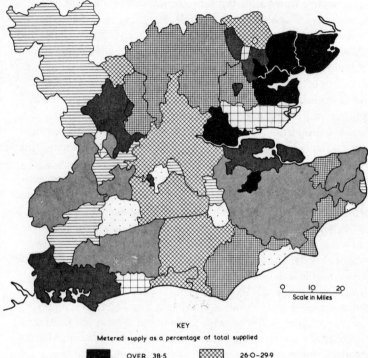

KEY

Metered supply as a percentage of total supplied

| | | | |
|---|---|---|---|
| ■ | OVER 38·5 | ▨ | 26·0–29·9 |
| ▨ | 34·0–38·5 | ▤ | 22·0–25·9 |
| ▨ | 32·0–33·9 | ▥ | 17·5–21·9 |
| ▦ | 30·0–31·9 | ░ | UNDER 17·5 |

## MAP 6   METERED SUPPLY AS A PERCENTAGE
## OF TOTAL SUPPLIED BY THE WATER UNDERTAKINGS

areas. It was not possible to find out how many people were employed in each area, but if such figures were available it is probable that a frequency distribution showing metered water per employee would have an even more marked mode. The range of values resulting from varying levels of commuting or employment participation rates would be removed.

Although the level of private abstraction also varies positively with the degree of urban development in a region, many firms requiring water for processing and cooling have found that it is not available within the urban area itself. Therefore quantity and occasionally quality requirements have

pushed some large water-using firms into surrounding rural areas where
abstraction sites are available. For example, Sant has found that paper and
board manufacture is one of the most rural industries in Britain, a feature
which is at least in part due to the industry's water requirements (98).

The density of manufacturing employment cannot explain the whole
spatial pattern of metered water consumption; also important is the
position of manufacturing in the total employment structure of an area.
For example, retirement, holiday and commuting areas often have a
relatively low proportion of residents employed in local manufacturing
industry, and so they have lower than average use of metered water. This
feature can be seen on maps 5 and 6; undertakings such as Windsor,
Epsom, Tunbridge Wells, Worthing and Hastings supply below average
quantities of metered water per resident and have metered water as a small
proportion of their total supply. On the other hand many of the
authorities with above average metered water use per resident, and with
metered water accounting for over 30% of total supply, are located in
two industrial belts. The first of these follows the axis of the Thames from
London eastwards into Essex and Kent, and the second stretches north
west from London through Uxbridge, Slough, Rickmansworth and
Watford to Luton. Two other areas, north-east Essex and Portsmouth
also emerge with high values on maps 5 and 6, but these result from the
metering of non-manufacturing units. For example, the Tendring Hundred
Waterworks Company (see key map 3) meters all premises and sites
catering for the large influx of summer visitors. This authority, together
with Colchester Rural District, Witham and Maldon, also meters
horticultural units. The high value for Portsmouth largely stems from
the sale of water on the meter to the naval dockyards, as 'ships in port
require high quality water for refilling cleaned boilers, distillation and
other equipment' (54 p 31).

There is a correspondence between the belts of high metered water
use, which appear on maps 5 and 6, and the areas where abstraction points
are concentrated; these are shown on map 2. This suggests that similar
factors may be influencing both the consumption of metered and privately
abstracted water. Certainly it would appear that the industry mix is one
of the factors determining the spatial pattern of metered water use, and
it was also one of the important determinants of the level of private
abstraction. It was found that many large private abstractors also
purchase large quantities of water from the local undertakings. For
example public utilities, oil refineries, and paper producers buy potable
metered supplies of water for staff hygiene, boiler make-up and

occasionally for use in the manufacturing process. Using the responses to the 'Industrial Survey' it was possible to test whether firms generally purchased large quantities of water from the local undertakings if they also abstracted large gallonages privately. From the regression analysis it appears that firms in the food, chemical and metal groups show a clear tendency for the quantity of purchased water to vary positively and significantly[7] with the level of private abstraction. On the other hand in the non-metallic minerals group the relationship between purchases and abstractions was negative, which infers that the greater is the gallonage of water abstracted, the smaller will be the firms' demand for potable water. This feature is the result of some sand and gravel workers abstracting large gallonages of water to pump the workings dry, while taking little if any water from local undertakings.

## Determinants of water usage within the firm

1. *Variables used in the analysis*
The broad spatial patterns of industrial water use are created by agglomerations of single water-using manufacturing units, and so the next stage in the analysis must be to consider what factors account for the variation in the quantity of water taken by individual firms. From the study of the spatial distributions it would appear that the number of persons employed, and the type of manufacturing taking place might be two worthwhile independent explanatory variables of a firm's water consumption. It is not, however, possible to include industry group in a regression equation as a variable, since no meaningful numerical value can be assigned to it. The regularity with which primary processing and other 'heavy' industry types emerged as large water users in the spatial analysis, did, however, suggest that the tonnage of raw materials entering the manufacturing process might be a useful proxy for industry group. For tonnage to be a useful surrogate the variation in the quantity of raw materials used must be significantly greater between industry groups than within them; unfortunately this did not prove to be the case as table 3 shows. Repeatedly the mean of one group falls within the standard deviations of the others, making ton-input valueless as a proxy for industry group, although in fact it did prove a useful explanatory variable of water consumption by firms. It was found that the only satisfactory way of analysing the influence of manufacturing type on the quantity of water taken was to sub-divide the respondent firms into industry groups, and

**Table 3.    Tonnage Input by Industry Group**

| Industry Group | Mean Ton-Input in '000 tons | Standard Deviation |
|---|---|---|
| Food | 75.82 | 172.06 |
| Drink | 64.12 | 43.19 |
| Plastics | 17.54 | 30.15 |
| Paper | 52.23 | 85.73 |
| Chemicals | 204.36 | 1413.44 |
| Non-Metallic Minerals | 137.60 | 278.96 |
| Metals | 59.23 | 165.39 |
| Engineering | 3.54 | 6.63 |

then to run separate regressions on each. The results which were obtained by doing this are discussed in Chapter 4.

It was thought that a third significant variable in the explanation of the quantity of water used would be the length of time that a firm, or its main plant, had occupied its present site without rebuilding (hereafter referred to as the 'age' of a firm). Old-established firms, with less efficient processing and cooling equipment, might well take relatively more water than modern firms with similar functional and size characteristics. Conversely, it has been argued that many of the newer and expanding industries are those with heavy demands for water; plastics, rubber, chemicals, oil refining and the public utilities are the most commonly quoted examples (97 p 55). If in the regression analysis a relationship between a firm's age and the quantity of water taken is established the sign of the regression coefficient will determine which of these two forces is the dominant one. On the other hand, if no relationship emerges it must be assumed that they cancel each other out.

Finally, two cost variables were added to the regression equations, namely the price at which water was purchased from the local undertaking, and the cost of obtaining water privately by abstraction. Hitherto, in Britain, it has generally been assumed that the quantity of water used is unresponsive to price changes, and is related only to the manufacturing characteristics of a firm (103 p 231) (124 (a) p 11). If this is so, no significant relationship between price and quantity will be found during the computations.

The remainder of this chapter will be concerned with investigating the effects of these five variables, employment, tonnage-input, age of plant, price of bought supplies and cost of abstracted supplies, on the quantity of water purchased by firms and privately abstracted by them. At this stage no division of the firms into manufacturing type groups will be made.

## 2 *Statistical problems*
In the analysis the computational method used was least-squares regression, and care has been taken in setting up the equation forms to ensure that the assumptions underlying this technique are fulfilled as far as possible. Any deviation from the assumptions must be taken into account in assessing the results. One of the estimation problems has already been discussed, namely the non-availability of a proxy or dummy variable for industry group; there are in addition three others.

Firstly, there is the problem of intercorrelation among particular explanatory variables in the regression models (65 p 201). The effects of this are to bias the parameter estimates, and to lower the overall levels of significance'by increasing the standard errors relative to the parameter estimates. On studying the correlation matrices of the independent variables it was found that multicollinearity probably existed between the number of persons employed and the tonnage of raw materials used. (See table 4.)

**Table 4.   Multicollinearity between Employment and Ton-Input**

| Industry Group | 'r' value between ton-input and employment |
|---|---|
| All firms: Total | 0.28 |
| Food | 0.80* |
| Drink | 0.50* |
| Paper and paper products | 0.86* |
| Plastics and Rubber | 0.12 |
| Chemicals | 0.69* |
| Non-metallic minerals | 0.10 |
| Metals and metal products | 0.08 |
| Engineering | 0.10 |
| 'Other' | 0.78* |

*'r' values at which the relationship *may* be great enough to affect the regression parameters.

While no single 'r' value is generally accepted as being the level at which multicollinearity begins to affect significantly the regression results, it is highly unlikely that values under 0.40 will present a problem (65 pp 201-7) (10 p 284). Multicollinearity is, therefore, unlikely to affect the results for industry as a whole, or for the plastics, non-metallic minerals, metals and engineering sub-groups. In the food, drink, paper, chemicals and 'other' groups, however, it is *possible* that the inclusion of employment and tonnage in one regression equation would increase the standard errors. Separate equation forms are therefore used wherever possible in these five sub-groups.

The second problem is usually referred to by econometricians as the 'identification problem' (70 p 92) (65 p 243). This arises out of the possibility that the relationship which is actually estimated may not in fact be the one which was intended. The best means of exemplifying this is by referring to an actual case that arises in this study. Price and quantity figures obtained from the sample firms were used in the estimation of a demand curve for purchased water. It is, however, possible that since a supply curve is also a relationship between price and quantity, it is this curve that has been estimated, not the demand curve. The problem is made more acute as some water undertakings reduce the price charged to supply each 1000 gallons of water to very large water users. There is also a possibility that the established relationship may be a hybrid form of the demand and supply curves.

**Figure 4 The identification problem**

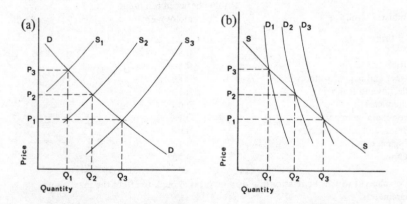

Figure 4 illustrates the identification problem and shows three sets of price and quantity data obtained from manufacturing units. In diagram (a) it is assumed that each firm is faced by a different supply curve for water and so the regression line here will be the demand curve. The second diagram, however, assumes that each firm has a different demand

curve and so the calculations will estimate the supply curve. As the
'Industrial Survey' includes a considerable number of different water
undertakings all with their own supply curves, the case for it being the
demand curve that is estimated is strengthened. On the other hand, there
is a considerable variation in the demand curves of individual firms, and
so the position is far from clear cut, with the strong possibility of the
relationship being a hybrid one, especially when the regressions are run
for industry as a whole. On subdividing industry into functional groups,
however, any wide variation in the slopes of the estimated curves between
groups is most likely to be attributable to differences in the demand curve.
The reason for this is that in a random sample the supply curves for each
industry group are likely to be similar and not the cause of large slope
variations. The regression results of the attempt to derive a demand curve
for industry as a whole must then be treated with care, and predictions
based upon them may be subject to error. It is thought, however, that the
demand curves estimated for the separate industry groups may be accepted
with reasonable confidence.

A final problem is that of autocorrelation, which is defined as
'correlation between the successive values of the error terms in the
regression equation' (65 p 177). The assumptions underlying least-squares
regression require that no such correlation exists. One cause of autocorrelation is the omission of an important explanatory variable from
the equation form. Each regression equation was tested for this feature
by using the Durbin-Watson Statistic, and rarely did it prove to be a
problem (29 a and b).

### 3 Results of the quantity regressions for industry as a whole

#### a Quantity of water purchased from local undertakings

A series of regressions was run to investigate the relationships between the
previously mentioned independent variables and the quantity of water
bought by each firm. At first all the regression equations used were
simple (i.e. one independent variable was used), then any significant
explanatory variables were incorporated into a multiple regression model.
In the analysis both linear and curvilinear forms of the equation were
tried in order to obtain the best fit of the regression line to the data.
The equations were transformed into the various curvilinear forms by
logging or squaring either one or all of the variables used.

It soon became apparent that the age of a plant (or the length of
time it had occupied its present site) was not a significant factor in

explaining the quantity of water taken (table 5, C 5). This suggests that there has been no consistent uni-directional change over time in the amount of water purchased by manufacturing units. This result is rather an unexpected one in view of the number of factors which might have produced an increase in purchase over time. Firstly, there has been an increase in the general size of plants (36 p 10); secondly, hygiene standards within factories have improved; and finally, it has been claimed that there is a growing tendency for manufacturers to rely less on abstracted water and more on purchased supplies (103 p 236). It would seem probable that many old-established firms have renovated their premises and increased hygiene standards without completely rebuilding the plant. Although the age of a firm does not affect purchased water consumption by industry as a whole, no conclusion can yet be made on the role of technical change in influencing water usage. Most innovations have taken place in the fields of processing and cooling and as has been mentioned many firms obtain water privately for these two uses.

Although privately abstracted water is not a perfect substitute for potable purchased supplies in all industrial uses, some substitution is still possible. It was thought that there might be a tendency for the quantity of water purchased to rise as the cost of abstracting water privately increased. In fact no such price cross-effect emerged in the regression computations, as the level of purchased supplies was not significantly related to the cost of abstraction (table 5 F5).

The most significant relationship proved to be between the number of persons employed and the quantity of water bought. This result is in accordance with the findings of the spatial analysis that a close connection existed between areas of high metered water consumption and areas of urban concentration. The basic hygiene requirements per man, which usually do not vary materially between firms, probably accounts for the high significance of the relationship (table 5 A5), while the scatter of the residuals is due to the varying amounts of water bought per employee for use in process. Normal linear regression produced the best-fit result, with each additional employee adding a similar quantity of water to the total (i.e. the slope of the regression line is constant). The mean value for this per person increment is 67,768 gallons per annum,[8] although there is a wide range of values around this mean. In cases where the firm uses large quantities of metered water in the manufacturing process the mean figure will underestimate the quantity of purchased water per employee.

Tonnage of raw materials entering the manufacturing process also proved to be related significantly to the gallonage of water purchased

**Table 5.   Determinants of the quantity of water purchased by all firms**

| independent explanatory variables | best-fit equation form | regression coefficient | standard error | 'F' test value (significance level) | degrees of freedom | level of explanation $R^2$ |
|---|---|---|---|---|---|---|
| 1 | 2 | 3 | 4 | 5 | 6 | 7 |
| A employment | $Q = a + bE$ | 67.76 | 10.14 | 44.68 | 164 | 21.5% |
| B raw materials ton-input ('000 tons per annum) | $Q = a + b \log T$ | 16884.91 | 3866.26 | 19.07 | 164 | 17.8 |
| C age of the firm | $Q = a + bA$ | 7675.09 | 4299.21 | 3.19 | 164 | 1.5+ |
| D price of bought water ('d' per 1000 gallons) | $Q = a + bP$ | −546.83 | 243.72 | 5.30 | 164 | 3.0 |
| E price of metered water ('d' per 1000 gallons) | $\log Q = a + b \log P_m$ | −2.86 | 0.68 | 17.75 | 119 | 12.98 |
| F cost of abstraction ('d' per 1000 gallons) | $\log Q = a + b \log C$ | −0.54 | 0.31 | 3.15 | 164 | 1.3+ |
| G multiple regression using:—employment :—tonnage :—price | $\log Q = a + b \log E + c \log T + d \log P$ | 1.089 0.268 0.814 | 0.159 0.105 0.219 | 46.95 6.51 13.80 | 162 | 34.9% |

+Not significant at the 0.95 level of probability

Symbol key page xi

by firms (table 5 B5). It did not, however, correlate as closely as the employment figures. The best-fit equation form was quantity bought against the log of ton-input ($Q = a + b \log T$) which suggests that the increment in the quantity of water purchased will decrease as ton-input increases, although the increment will remain positive.

A final significant explanatory variable of the quantity of water taken from the statutory undertakings is the price paid per 1,000 gallons of supply (table 5 D5). In the first regression of price against quantity all the available observations were used, including both firms that were charged on rateable value and those that had a metered water supply. This computation produced a significant result, at the 0.95 level of probability,[9] but the degree of explanation ($R^2$) achieved was low. Firms that are charged on the rateable value of their premises do not pay a true unit price for the water they use, and so they are not influenced by price changes. It was therefore decided to re-run the regression omitting any firm that was not supplied on a meter. This improved both the level of significance and the $R^2$ value. Another important effect of omitting the unmetered values was to alter significantly the elasticity[10] of the demand curve for water (i.e. alter the slope of the regression line). In the first run the elasticity calculated about the means of the variables was −0.83; as this value is less than one, the demand curve was inelastic at that point. When a similar calculation was made on the results of the second regression the elasticity was −2.862, the curve is therefore highly elastic at the mean price and quantity. Although, as has been mentioned, these results must be viewed with caution due to the 'identification problem', it is likely that manufacturers are responsive to price changes. It is interesting to note that the curve becomes elastic as soon as unmetered firms are omitted which suggests that metering does reduce consumption. This result agrees with those obtained from calculations on American and European data (37 p 620).

Throughout these regressions the $R^2$ values are low, which means that any attempts to predict from the results would be subject to large errors. Although significant relationships have been found to exist, they do not explain much of the variation observed between firms in the quantity of water purchased. In fact a wide scatter of observations around the regression line is inevitable with such a polyglot group of industries; the levels of explanation are greatly improved when the firms are divided into industry groups (Chapter 4).

A model containing price, employment, and tonnage of raw materials could only explain 35% of the variation in the quantity of water purchased

Table 6.  Determinants of the quantity of water privately abstracted by all firms

| independent explanatory variables 1 | best-fit equation form 2 | regression coefficient 3 | standard error 4 | 'f' test value (significance level) 5 | degrees of freedom 6 | level of explanation ($R^2$) 7 |
|---|---|---|---|---|---|---|
| A employment | $QA = a + b\,E$ | 385.06 | 146.00 | 6.96 | 164 | 4.1% |
| B raw materials ton-input ('000 tons p.a.) | $QA = a + b \log T$ | 101614.33 | 53367.33 | 3.63 | 164 | 2.2 |
| C age of firm | $QA = a + b \log A$ | −9167.03 | 60907.2 | 0.02 | 164 | 0 + |
| D price of purchased water | $\log QA = a + b\,P$ | −0.0252 | 0.0128 | 3.84 | 164 | 3.0 |
| E cost of abstraction | $\log QA = a + b \log C$ | 1.74914 | 0.62882 | 7.74 | 164 | 4.1 |
| F multiple regression equation {employment tonnage price cost} | $\log QA = a + b \log E +$ $c \log T + d \log P + e \log C$ | 0.7465 0.29229 −0.73315 1.7491 | 0.3287 0.21757 0.4529 0.6288 | 5.16 1.80 2.62 7.74 | 161 | 16.6% + |

+not significant at 0.95 level of probability

by all firms. The absence of autocorrelation does suggest, however, that
no other independent variables cause the residuals to be serially related.
Multicollinearity between the explanatory variables was not present, and
so the results are free from this source of inaccuracy.

b Quantity of water abstracted from private sources

A similar series of regressions was run using the quantity of water
abstracted privately by each firm as the dependent variable. The results
of these computations are shown in table 6.

The age of the plant again proved an insignificant determinant of
level of water consumption, and it added nothing to the level of
explanation (table 6 C5 and C7). For industry as a whole there is no
dominant time trend in the quantity of water abstracted privately
per manufacturing unit. It would appear that factors tending to cause
a decline in private abstraction per firm, such as technological advances
in water-using equipment (6 p 476) or the increasing scarcity of
abstraction sites have been counterbalanced by forces leading to rising
abstraction. One such factor causing an increasing demand for privately
abstracted supplies may be the tendency for some modern growth
industries to be large water users (47 p 145). For example, the
development of oil-refining capacity in south east England has greatly
increased private abstraction of water, especially from the Thames
estuary.

All other independent variables proved significant at the 0.95 level
of probability. Abstraction costs emerged as the variable with the
highest 'F' test value (i.e. the highest significance) but it is unlikely
that the relationship established by the regression is a *demand* curve
for privately abstracted water. The positive sign of the regression
coefficient suggests that the log-log curve is a *supply* function rather than
a demand curve; as more water is made available the marginal costs
of supply increase. Manufacturers only pay (or think they pay) a mean
price of 1.3 pence per 1,000 gallons for abstracted water, and therefore
it is probable that the cost rarely enters into their estimates of water
requirements. Availability is likely to be a more important factor than
pumping costs in explaining the variation between firms in the quantity
of water abstracted privately. It is, however, possible that abstractors may
become responsive to cost changes at higher cost levels; for example the
new charges on each 1,000 gallons withdrawn may well be high enough to
decrease the quantity taken.

Employment emerged as another significant explanatory variable, but

**Table 7.  Determinants of the total quantity of water taken by all firms**

| independent explanatory variables 1 | best-fit equation form 2 | regression coefficient 3 | standard error 4 | 'f' test value (significance level) 5 | degrees of freedom 6 | level of explanation ($R^2$) 7 |
|---|---|---|---|---|---|---|
| A employment | $\log Qt = a + b \log E$ | 1.2105 | 0.1558 | 60.38 | 164 | 20.0% |
| B raw material ton-input ('000 tons p.a.) | $Qt = a + b\,T$ | 994.949 | 102.088 | 90.98 | 164 | 36.8 |
| C age of firm | $Qt = a + b\,A$ | 21227.29 | 52085.0 | 0.17 | 164 | 0.1 + |
| D price of bought water | $\log Qt = a + b\,P$ | −0.0257 | 0.00693 | 13.74 | 164 | 7.2 |
| E cost of abstraction | $\log Qt = a + b \log C$ | 0.2243 | 0.29806 | 0.57 | 164 | 0.2 + |
| F multiple regression model { employment | $\log Qt = a + b \log E$ | 1.2105 | 0.1558 | 60.38 | 162 | 47.3 |
| tonnage | $+ c \log T + d \log P$ | 0.4509 | 0.1031 | 19.11 | | |
| price | | −0.5982 | 0.2147 | 7.77 | | |

+Not significant at 0.95 level of probability

it is not as closely correlated with the level of abstraction as it was with the quantity of water purchased. When employment is used to explain variations between firms in the amounts of water taken from private sources, it probably acts solely as a size variable; the larger the labour force, the larger the firm and the more water is required for process and cooling. This generalization does not always hold as some firms are able to substitute capital for labour. Throughout the regression on the quantity of water purchased, employment not only acted as a size variable but it also isolated one important industrial use of water, namely sanitation.

The tonnage of raw materials entering the manufacturing process was only just significantly related to the quantity of water abstracted by all firms. This low significance and the low $R^2$ value results from the fact that the regression line is made up of a combination of curves, a separate curve for each industry group.

Throughout the computations on the quantity of water abstracted the levels of explanation achieved were low. In fact a multiple regression model that included price, cost, employment and ton-input explained only 16.6% of the variation between firms in the quantity of water abstracted. The results cannot be used for prediction.

c Total water used by firms

Finally the regressions were repeated using the total amount of water used by each firm as the dependent variable (table 7). Three independent variables achieved significance, employment, tonnage and the price of bought supplies. A multiple regression model including these three variables explained 47.3% of the variation in total industrial water usage. Throughout the total computations the significance and $R^2$ levels showed an improvement over those achieved in the purchased water and abstracted water regressions. It would appear that the total amount of water used varies relatively systematically with these explanatory variables, whereas the distribution of this total between metered and private supplies is subject to influence from more random elements. Much of the unexplained differences in usage probably stem from the type of manufacturing engaged in by the sample firms, and this will be considered in the following chapter.

# Chapter 4

# Inter-industry variations in the demand for water

In the previous chapter it was stated that a large proportion of the unexplained variation in the quantity of water demanded by manufacturers is probably due to the variety of industry groups in the sample. As no dummy or proxy variable is available for industry group, it is necessary to subdivide the firms into manufacturing types in order to isolate the effect of process variation on water consumption. In this chapter an attempt will be made to analyse the variation between industry groups in the uses to which water is put, and in the sources from which demand for water is satisfied. The independent variables, employment, tonnage of raw material inputs, age of firm, price of bought water, and abstraction costs, will then be used to explain some of the inter- and intra-industry differences in the demand for water.

### Inter-industry variation in the uses of water (table 8)

Some firms were unable or unwilling to specify what proportion of the total water taken was used for each industrial purpose. As some industry groups contained very few firms able to provide this information it was not possible to estimate accurately inter-industry variations in the proportion of total water used for cooling, sanitation, processing and so on. It was, however, possible to find how many firms in each manufacturing group took water for each of these purposes.

Water is required for staff hygiene by virtually every firm in every industry group, but it is doubtful whether this use accounts for the greatest quantity of water demanded in any group. One possible exception to this is the printing industry, in which very little water is taken for any other purpose. The non-metallic minerals group contained the greatest number of firms (3) which claimed not to use water for sanitation. As all firms in the 'Industrial Survey' were asked to complete the questionnaire for their main plant, it is possible that these three manufacturers have answered for a mineral working, where running water for staff hygiene may well not be provided.[1]

Although most firms require water for sanitation, irrespective of the type of production, there are wide differences between industry groups in the proportion of firms taking water for cooling (table 8 column 2). On the one hand all drink manufacturers demand a supply of cooling water, as do over 60% of respondents in the food, furniture, chemicals, metals and mechanical engineering groups. Conversely, no firms in the clothing and leather industries required cooling water. In the paper group as a whole, 50% of the respondents took a supply for cooling, but it was found that whereas every raw paper producer required such a supply very few paper product manufacturers made similar demands. In the same way it was found that all raw plastic and rubber manufacturers required water for cooling, but secondary product producers in the same industry group did not take any water for this purpose.

Inter-industry variations in the proportion of firms using water to produce steam are also large (table 8 column 5). All respondents in the drink, leather and furniture groups demanded a high quality supply of water for boiler feed purposes. Similarly, over 70% of firms in the food, paper, plastics and chemical industries also required water for steam raising. The smallest proportion of firms (40%) receiving a supply for this purpose occurred in the mechanical engineering group. In every industry group the absolute quantity of water demanded for steam raising was small, but the quality requirements were often stringent.

The proportion of firms taking water for use in the actual manufacturing process also varies greatly between industry groups. Every respondent in the drink and leather industries and over 70% of firms producing food, furniture, paper, chemicals and non-metallic minerals used water in process. On the other hand, very few firms in the precision engineering (37%) and in the clothing (20%) groups made use of water in this way. It was found that only two firms in the clothing group, both of which manufactured textiles, used process water but these demands accounted for over 95% of the total water consumption of the industry group.

Water for cleaning materials, plant and vehicles is another common requirement in some industry groups, for example all printing firms took a supply for cleaning, as did 89% of the respondents in the drink industry. The use was of least importance in the mechanical engineering and plastics groups in which only 14% and 18% respectively of firms required cleaning water. Other uses of water include fire-fighting, which is most important in the furniture and timber industry, conveying of materials in solution or suspension, for example cement slurry, and the testing of equipment such as pumps.

Table 8.   Inter-industry variation in the uses of water

| industry group 1 | cooling 2 % | washing plant and materials 3 % | in process 4 % | steam raising 5 % | staff hygiene 6 % | 'other' 7 % |
|---|---|---|---|---|---|---|
| A food | 64.7 | 64.7 | 76.5 | 88.2 | 100 | 29.3 |
| B drink | 100 | 88.9 | 100 | 100 | 100 | 44.4 |
| C clothing and textiles | 0 | 40 | 20 | 60 | 100 | 20 |
| D leather and fur | 0 | 25 | 100 | 100 | 100 | 0 |
| E furniture and timber | 57.2 | 14.3 | 71.4 | 100 | 100 | 57.2 |
| F paper and paper products | 50 | 36.4 | 77.3 | 86.4 | 95.5 | 13.6 |
| G printing | 75 | 100 | 50 | 50 | 100 | 0 |
| H plastics and rubber | 54.5 | 18.2 | 54.5 | 72.7 | 100 | 18.2 |
| I chemicals | 76.0 | 40.0 | 82.0 | 76.0 | 100 | 16.0 |
| J non-metallic minerals | 26.7 | 46.7 | 73.3 | 46.7 | 80.1 | 13.2 |
| K metal and metal products | 84.6 | 38.5 | 61.5 | 53.8 | 92.3 | 30.8 |
| L mechanical engineering | 57.2 | 14.3 | 57.2 | 42.9 | 100 | 14.3 |
| M precision engineering | 50.0 | 75.0 | 37.5 | 62.5 | 100 | 12.5 |

percentage of firms* taking water for each of the following uses

*only firms answering part two of the questionnaire are included in this table. For actual numbers see Appendix A.

## Inter-industry variation in the sources of water supplies

In the previous chapter it was seen that the vast majority of firms take at
least part of their water requirements from local undertakings. Rarely will
a firm use privately abstracted ground water for staff hygiene purposes,
although a few exceptions do exist amongst paper manufacturers and
non-metallic mineral producers located in Kent. These firms usually
abstract water from the chalk where the level of treatment necessary to
produce a potable quality is minimal; in addition the firms have treatment
equipment already installed to obtain a high quality process or boiler-feed
water. The proportion of firms relying *solely* on purchased supplies varies
with the type of manufacturing, being greatest in the printing group in
which no firm abstracts water privately, and in the clothing industry in
which only 9% of firms own a private source of supply. It is noticeable
that in no industry group do respondents with private supplies outnumber
those which take all their requirements from local water undertakings. The
paper and food industries have the greatest proportions of private
abstractors, 43% and 32% respectively, but in the other groups only
between 10% and 20% of respondents did not rely solely on the public
water supply undertakings.

Although a minority of respondents in each industry group obtain
water from private sources, these firms are responsible for the bulk of
water consumption in most groups. In gallonage terms private abstraction
is an important source of industrial water in all but three industry groups.
These three groups are printing, which has no private abstractors, drink,
in which 98% of the water used by the respondents is obtained from
public supply undertakings, and metal products, which only takes 10%
of its water from private sources. Although the fact that drink producers
require a high quality potable water for incorporation into the product
increases the importance of purchased supplies, it is known that the
proportion of water abstracted by firms in this industry has been
underestimated. Brewers, most of whom own private water supply sources,
were most reluctant to complete the 'Industrial Survey' questionnaire and
this has caused a marked bias towards the small drink producers, who
rely on bought water supplies. From the abstraction licences of right for
south east England it was found that the average amount of water
abstracted privately by non-respondent drink manufacturers is 33.817
mgy, whereas the respondents only take an average of 1.198 mgy. The
low percentage of abstracted water in the total quantity taken by the
metal and metal products industry probably only represents the situation
in south east England, where primary metal manufacturers are relatively

rare. It is likely that over Britain as a whole purchased water would account for a far smaller proportion of the total quantity used by the industry than it does in the south east.

In most of the other industry groups over 80% of the total water requirements are obtained from private sources, for example clothing (98%), leather (93%) and chemicals (90%). Firms engaged in the primary processing stages of manufacture are usually the ones which abstract large gallonages of water. Water appears to be used in the greatest quantities when the manufacturing process changes the physical constitution of a raw material. On the other hand the later stages of manufacture only change the form of the material inputs, and water is rarely needed in large quantities for processing or in cooling. For example, raw paper production involves the conversion of pulp, wastepaper or rags into paper, whereas the manufacture of paper products involves shaping, cutting and printing. In the same way metal manufacture involves the conversion of ores into metals and alloys, whereas the production of metal goods involves merely a change in the form which the metal takes. Similar examples of the split between a large water-using primary processing stage of manufacture and a low water-using secondary stage occur in the leather, chemicals, clothing and plastics groups. It must be stressed that firms engaged in primary processing and abstracting large gallonages of water are a small minority in every industry group. For example in the clothing and textile group only one respondent had a private source of supply but this firm accounted for 98% of the total water used in the group.

Abstractions from wells and bores are more *numerous* than from surface sources, but in terms of the *quantity* of water taken the latter. are more important. In four industry groups, drink, leather, mechanical engineering and precision engineering, more water is obtained from ground water than from surface sources, but in all these groups the quantity abstracted in total is relatively small. The largest gallonages of water are taken by firms in the paper and chemical industries; abstractions are normally from low quality sources such as rivers or estuaries. It is usual for the bulk of water to be used by these firms for cooling and most of it is returned to source with little diminution in quality. Most abstractors obtain their surface water from rivers or tidal estuaries, although some firms pump from canals and gravel pits. Two rather unusual sources of supply did emerge in the sample survey. One metal products firm uses water from an outfall sewer, and a plastics manufacturer purchased water from a neighbouring abstractor.

Table 9.   Inter-industry variation in the quantity of water demanded

| | purchased water | | | | |
|---|---|---|---|---|---|
| | 1 | 2 | 3 | 4 | 5 |
| | unrecorded and under 100,000 | 100,000 to 499,999 | 500,000 gpa to 1.999 | 2 to 9.999 | over 10 |
| industry group | gpa | gpa | mgy | mgy | mgy |
| | % | % | % | % | % |
| food | 2.2 | 5.0 | 15.5 | – | 57.5 |
| drink | 11.1 | – | 11.1 | – | 77.7 |
| clothing and textiles | 82.8 | 8.6 | 8.6 | – | – |
| leather and fur | 57.0 | 14.0 | 29.0 | – | – |
| furniture and timber | 58.3 | 24.9 | 8.4 | 8.4 | – |
| paper and paper products | 37.0 | 6.6 | 13.2 | 19.9 | 23.3 |
| printing | 50.0 | 12.5 | 12.5 | 25.0 | – |
| plastic and rubber | 44.4 | – | 11.1 | 27.6 | 16.5 |
| chemicals | 23.0 | 4.9 | 18.6 | 27.8 | 25.7 |
| non-metallic minerals | 39.0 | 5.5 | 22.2 | 22.2 | 11.1 |
| metals and metal products | 52.0 | – | 24.0 | 8.0 | 16.0 |
| mechanical engineering | 68.4 | 7.8 | 7.8 | 7.8 | 7.8 |
| precision engineering | 46.6 | 20.1 | 20.1 | 6.7 | 6.7 |

Some of the firms sampled during the 'Industrial Survey' expressed a willingness to receive a non-potable supply of water from their local undertaking at a price per 1000 gallons lower than that paid for drinking water. The quantity of water demanded would, however, depend upon the price charged by the undertakings. There appear to be two categories of firms which could provide a market for a publically supplied non-potable water. Firstly, there are a number of firms already using purchased potable water in process and for cooling, for example firms in the furniture, timber and non-metallic minerals groups, where the quality of process water is not important as it does not come into contact with an edible product. 80% of the furniture and timber firms in the survey were interested in receiving a piped non-potable water supply as were 53% of non metallic mineral producers. Some furniture manufacturers pointed out that stand-by water to be used in the case of fire could also be non-potable. A second category of firms which may purchase this water quality are those which are unable or unwilling to locate or relocate to a suitable abstraction site. It is possible that this group will increase in importance as control over abstractions becomes more severe, and as the costs of abstraction rise with the newly introduced gallonage charges.

| | privately abstracted water | | | | | total water taken | | | |
| 6 | 7 | 8 | 9 | 10 | 11 | 12 | 13 | 14 | 15 |
| no private abstraction | under 499,999 gpa | 500,000 gpa to 1.999 mgy | 2 to 9.999 mgy | over 10 mgy | unrecorded and under 99,999 gpa | 100,000 to under 499,999 gpa | 500,000 gpa to 1.999 mgy | 2 to 9.999 mgy | over 10 mgy |
|---|---|---|---|---|---|---|---|---|---|
| % | % | % | % | % | % | % | % | % | % |
| 68.4 | – | 5.3 | – | 26.3 | 22.0 | 5.0 | 15.5 | – | 57.5 |
| 77.7 | – | – | 11.1 | 11.1 | 11.1 | – | – | 11.1 | 77.7 |
| 91.4 | – | – | – | 8.6 | 82.8 | 8.6 | – | – | 8.6 |
| 71.4 | – | – | – | 28.6 | 57.0 | – | 14.0 | – | 29.0 |
| 83.4 | – | – | 8.4 | 8.4 | 58.3 | 16.8 | 8.4 | 16.8 | 8.4 |
| 56.6 | – | – | 3.5 | 39.9 | 26.6 | 6.6 | 9.9 | 9.9 | 47.0 |
| 100.0 | – | – | – | – | 50.0 | 12.5 | 12.5 | 25.0 | – |
| 78.0 | – | – | 11.1 | 11.1 | 14.4 | – | 11.1 | 22.2 | 22.2 |
| 88.4 | 1.6 | 1.6 | 1.6 | 8.0 | 23.0 | 3.7 | 17.9 | 26.1 | 29.3 |
| 72.5 | 16.6 | – | – | 11.1 | 22.2 | 16.6 | 22.2 | 22.2 | 16.6 |
| 84.0 | 8.0 | – | 8.0 | – | 52.0 | – | 24.0 | 8.0 | 16.0 |
| 76.6 | – | – | 15.6 | 7.8 | 46.4 | 7.8 | 7.8 | 23.4 | 15.6 |
| 86.4 | – | 6.7 | – | 6.7 | 46.6 | 20.1 | 13.5 | 6.7 | 13.5 |

**Inter-industry variation in the quantity of water demanded (table 9)**
Table 9 shows the percentage distribution of firms by the quantity of
water taken. Each cell of the table shows the percentage of firms in a
given industry group which takes a given quantity of water. For example
in the food sub-group 57.5% of the firms purchase over 10 mgy of water
from local undertakings (A 5). Using this table the inter-industry variations
in the quantities of water purchased, privately abstracted and taken in
total were studied.

1 *Purchased water supplies*
One interesting feature to emerge from this part of the table is the large
variation between manufacturing types in the proportion of firms taking
very small quantities of water below 100,000 gy and only completing
the first section of the questionnaire (Column 1). In these cases water
is of no importance either as a locational or a cost factor. Industries which
are comprised of predominantly small, labour intensive firms usually have
a high proportion of firms in this category. For example, in the clothing
industry 82.8% of the respondents purchase under 100,000 gallons of
water from the local undertakings, and in fact the only firms taking over

this quantity were textile producers. The furniture, leather, printing and mechanical engineering groups also have a large proportion of firms in this lowest quantity category. On the other hand, industries, such as drink, food and chemicals, which require potable water for use in the manufacturing process as well as for staff hygiene, have only a small proportion of firms purchasing under 100,000 gpy. In the paper industry there is a clear bi-modal distribution with paper product firms purchasing small gallonages of water and raw paper manufacturers usually purchasing over 1 mgy. The only raw paper producers in the under 100,000 gallons category in fact do not purchase any water at all; they rely solely on private abstraction.

At the other end of the quantity purchased scale the food and drink industries stand out with the largest percentage of firms taking over 10 mgy of water from local undertakings. Large gallonages are purchased by firms in these two groups as water enters or comes into contact with an edible product. This increases the amount of water obtained by purchase relative to the quantity abstracted privately. The same need for potability may also explain the large proportion of chemical firms taking over 2 mgy (Col 4 & 5). A rather different factor possibly explains the high percentage of firms in the paper industry which purchase large gallonages of water. It is likely that bought water is used to make up deficiencies in the quantity or quality of water privately abstracted by raw paper producers. For example, three of the respondent raw paper manufacturers reported increased purchases of water from the local authorities to compensate for the pollution of their ground water. High quality paper production requires relatively pure process water and the costs of removing salt impurities can be greater than the price charged by water undertakings.[2]

As to be expected those industry groups with a high percentage of firms in the lowest quantity category were also those with few firms purchasing large gallonages of water; the percentage of firms in each quantity cell decreases as the amount of water purchased increases. For example the clothing, leather, furniture and printing groups have no respondent firms taking over 10 mgy and both the engineering groups have less than 9% of firms falling in this category.

*2 Abstracted supplies (table 9)*
One of the most noticeable features in the section of table 9 which shows the quantity of water abstracted privately, is that only a small proportion of firms with private sources of supply take less than 2 million gallons a year. Firms requiring less than this gallonage would be unlikely to recover

the costs of locating to an abstraction point, and of purchasing, installing and running pumping and cleaning equipment; therefore it is usual for most firms requiring less than 2 mgy to obtain all their water by purchase from the local undertakings. This feature was borne out in the regression analysis on the determinants of the demand for water, as in some industry groups there was a threshold quantity of water used before private abstraction became an economic proposition. Alternatively, in some other industries the firms had to reach a threshold size (measured by the number of persons employed or by the tonnage of raw materials used) before private abstraction became worthwhile. It was found that the majority of abstractors pump well over 10 mgy, while the highest recorded quantities are over 10,000 mgy.

The proportion of non-abstractors (column 6) is lowest in the paper (56.6%) and the food (68%) industries. In no group do abstractors outnumber those firms relying solely on purchased supplies, although, as has been seen, in terms of the quantity of water taken private abstraction is by far the most important source of supply in most industry groups. Although only 33% of the respondent drink producers owned a private water supply source, it is possible that this figure underestimates the proportion of abstractors in the industry. When the abstraction licence registers were analysed it was found that approximately 54% of drink manufacturers in the south east abstract some proportion of their water requirements from private sources. The discrepancy between the two percentages is caused by the reluctance of brewers to answer the 'Industry Survey' questionnaire; this has been discussed on page

In some of the industry groups the occurrence of private abstraction differentiated between the various types of manufacturing process. For example, in the leather industry only firms undertaking the initial processing of hides find it worthwhile having a private water supply; the manufacturers of leather products rely solely on purchased supplies. Similarly textile firms take water by private abstraction, whereas clothing manufacturers purchase all their requirements, and paper product firms are distinguished from raw paper producers because they rarely own a private supply source.

## 3 Total supplies

The distributional patterns that emerge for the *total* water taken by firms will not be discussed in detail as most of the features have been mentioned above. If the quantity taken by purchase and private abstraction is used as a criterion of the importance of the resource to firms, then water is most

vital in the food, drink and paper industries, and it is of minor importance
to firms in the clothing, furniture and printing groups.

## The determinants of the quantity of water demanded

Nine industry groups were analysed in detail in an attempt to isolate
the factors which determine the quantity of water demanded by firms in
each of the groups. It was not possible to run regression computations for
each stratum of the 'Industrial Survey' as the number of firms able
to answer the section of the questionnaire on abstracted supplies was
limited in some of the smaller groups, and especially in those in which
water has negligible importance. In order to keep the degrees of freedom[3]
in the regression equations up to an acceptable level these smaller groups
were combined, putting like with like wherever possible. For example,
metal and metal product firms were formed into one group, and all
engineering concerns (whether mechanical, precision or electrical)
were combined into another. A composite group, referred to as 'other
industries' includes clothing and textiles, furniture and timber, fur and
printing firms; these are all labour-intensive types of manufacture and
they all require relatively small quantities of water.

By combining industry groups the levels of significance and explanation
obtained from the regression computations are inevitably decreased
because one line is being fitted to the observations when in reality
different regression lines exist for each manufacturing type. The scatter
of the observations around the one best-fit line is therefore increased.
On the other hand, when only a few observations are used the results of
a regression may be meaningless as the range of values around the
regression line will tend to be small. For example, a perfect linear
relationship must always exist if there are only two observations, and
with three or four observations a curvilinear equation form would produce
a good fit.

### 1 *Chemical Manufacture*[4]

Within this industry group the tonnage of raw materials used emerges as
the most important explanatory variable of the variation between firms
in the quantities of water purchased, privately abstracted and taken in
total. Table 10 clearly illustrates this feature; higher levels of explanation
($R^2$) (Column 8) and significance[5] were obtained when ton-input was used
as the independent variable. It would appear that the quantity of raw
materials used partially differentiates between the various chemical

**Table 10. Determinants of the quantity of water taken by chemical firms**

| dependent variable 1 | significant independent variables 2 | best-fit equation form 3 | regression coefficient (b) 4 | standard error 5 | 'f' test value (significance level) 6 | degrees of freedom 7 | level of explanation $(R^2)$ 8 |
|---|---|---|---|---|---|---|---|
| A purchased water | raw materials: tonnage | $Q^2 = a + bT$ | 15121172.5 | 510685.7 | 876.73 | 48 | 97.3% |
| | employment | $Q = a + bE^2$ | 0.03895 | 0.00528 | 54.44 | 48 | 53.1 |
| | price of metered water | $\log Q = a + bP_m$ | -0.0302 | 0.0145 | 4.312 | 35 | 10.9 |
| | multiple regression { price of bought water + quantity of water abstracted } | $\log Q = a + bP + \log QA$ | -2.05798 | 0.43887 | 21.99 | 47 | 37.0 |
| | | | 0.10626 | 0.06987 | 2.31 | | |
| B abstracted water | raw materials: ton-input | $QA = a + bT$ | 999.69 | 1.9119 | 273418.8 | 48 | 100 * |
| | employment | $QA = a + bE$ | 2115.56 | 318.86 | 44.03 | 48 | 47.8 |
| C total water taken | raw materials: ton-input | $Qt = a + bT$ | 994.216 | 4.232 | 55184.6 | 48 | 100 * |
| | employment | $Qt = a + bE$ | 2122.52 | 317.196 | 44.78 | 48 | 48.3 |
| | price of bought water | $\log Qt = a + bP$ | -2.164 | 0.4389 | 46.22 | 48 | 34.1 |
| D purchased water | abstracted water | $Q^2 = a + bQA$ | 15501.85 | 371.53 | 1740.92 | 48 | 97.4 |

*The equation forms $QA^2$ (or $Qt$) = $a + bT$ also gave a 100% level of explanation, but for interpretive problems see text.
No multiple regression model using tonnage and employment was attempted due to multicollinearity.

processes, each of which has a different demand for water. For example, raw chemical production requires considerably more water than does pharmaceuticals.

The amount of water *purchased* from local water undertakings by chemical firms varies positively with the tonnage of raw materials used, although the shape of the best-fit equation, $Q^2 = a + bT$, implies that the rate of increase decreases as high levels of ton-input are reached. One possible explanation for the decreasing rate of increase at high tonnages is that more substitution of privately abstracted water for bought supplies occurs as demand increases. Firms using large amounts of raw materials and requiring large gallonages of water may take an increasing proportion of their needs from private sources. The simple regression equation with tonnage of raw materials as the sole independent variable explained 97.3% of the variation between chemical plants in the quantity of water purchased. As the regression constant[6] $a$ of this equation is positive there appears to be a threshold quantity of water purchased before any manufacturing occurs (i.e. before any tonnage of raw material is added). The threshold value may be interpreted as the minimum gallonage of water likely to be required by any profitable plant in this group; this minimum, which is approximately 557,000 gallons per annum, will be *purchased* irrespective of the type of processing occurring in the plant and of the tonnage of raw materials used.

It was found that the quantity of raw materials entering the manufacturing process also appears to be a good explanatory variable of the amount of water *abstracted privately* by chemical firms. When a regression analysis was undertaken using data supplied by all the respondents in the industry, the linear equation form $QA = a + bT$ appeared to explain all the variations between firms in the quantity of water abstracted, but the very high correlation ($r = .99995$) probably results because one very extreme observation has been included in the regression. This one firm is atypical of those in the group being a petro-chemical plant and oil refinery, which uses 10 million tons of raw materials each year and abstracts over 44,000 million gallons of water per annum. In comparison, the largest tonnage used by the other firms in the group is 6,000 tons, and the largest abstractor only takes 110 mgy. As the majority of chemical firms are all clustered at the lower end of the quantity axis the regression line for all practical purposes is between only two points, the cluster of relatively small abstractors and the one very large-scale water user. A highly significant result is therefore to be expected, but the slope of the regression line and the constant term of

**Figure 5. Negative and positive constant terms**

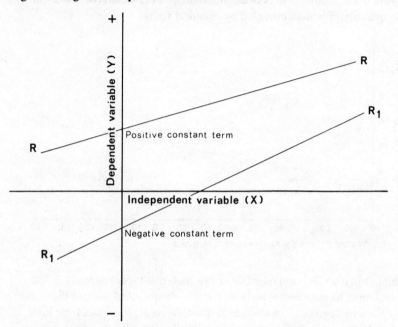

When the constant is positive the regression line crosses the 'Y' axis above zero
($R$ - $R$). When the constant is negative the 'Y' axis is intersected below zero
($R^1$ - $R^1$).

the equation cannot be applied to the majority of chemical firms.

This does not mean to say that the quantity of raw materials entering
the manufacturing process is not a good explanatory variable of the
gallonage of water taken from private sources by the relatively small
abstractors. In fact abstraction and tonnage were found to be closely and
significantly related. Most of the firms (40 of the respondents) in the
chemical group take between 2,000 and 3,500 tons of raw materials each
year and rarely do these firms use sufficient water in process and for
cooling to make private abstraction a worthwhile proposition. The
remaining 7 respondents in the chemical group all own private water
supply sources. They lay on or close to a line drawn from the cluster of
non-abstractors at a slope of 28 mgy per 1,000 tons (see figure 6). In
other words if a chemical plant uses 1,000 tons of raw materials more
than another it will probably also abstract approximately 28 mgy more
water. As the regression line cuts the tonnage axis at a positive value, it

**Figure 6 The relationship between the tonnage of raw materials used and the quantity of water abstracted by chemical firms**

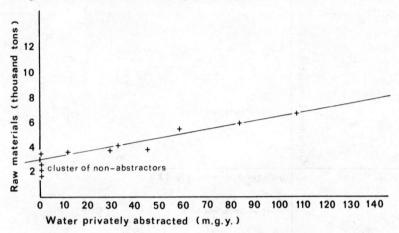

implies that a minimum quantity of raw materials (approximately 2,700 tons) must be used before sufficient water is required to warrant the location of the plant to a suitable abstraction point; purchases from local undertakings provide the relatively small gallonages of water more economically.

As abstracted supplies of water are responsible for a high proportion (90%) of the *total* quantity used by chemical plants it is to be expected that the best-fit regression lines and equation forms will be similar for abstracted and total supplies. In fact they have both been affected by the extreme value discussed earlier and the slopes of the two regression lines were not significantly different when statistically tested (66 p 29) (39 pp 237-41). One important difference between the two sets of results did emerge, however, as the regression line for the *total* quantity of water taken intersected the quantity axis at a negative value on the tonnage axis for the equation $Qt = a + bT$. The implication from this is that all chemical plants (or those employing over 15 persons) will *use* a minimum of approximately 686,000 gallons of water per annum taken both from private sources and from the public water suppliers.

Although the tonnage of raw materials was the best independent explanatory variable, both the number of persons employed and the price of *bought* supplies were also significantly related to the quantity of water used. Employment correlates most highly with the amount of water

*purchased* when a regression equation $Q = a + bE^2$ is used.[7] As the
relationship is a positive one the power function implies that the quantity
of water purchased increases at a greater rate as employment increases.
About the mean level of employment, which is 286.5 persons, the slope
of the regression line is 2.232, or in other words an increase of one
employee is associated with an increased demand for bought water of
approximately 2,200 gallons per annum, although there will be a scatter
of values around this figure. As employment rises above the mean level
the quantity of water added per employee will increase at an increasing
rate, while firms employing less than the mean number of workers will
demand less than 2,200 gallons per employee. The constant term of
this equation is positive and this implies that all chemical firms must
purchase a minimum quantity of water irrespective of the number of
persons employed.

Employment best explains the variation between firms in the quantities
of water *abstracted privately* and *taken in total* when a linear equation
form is used. As in the ton-input computations the regression coefficients
are virtually the same for both $QA = a + bE$, and $Qt = a + bE$; the $b$ values
being 2115.56 and 2122.51 respectively. In other words, in both cases the
quantity of water demanded will increase by approximately 2,100,000
gallons per annum for each additional employee.[8] There is, however, a
scatter of values around this level. The constant term is negative in both
equations. In the case of *private abstraction,* the sign of the constant is
explained by the fact that small firms are unlikely to require sufficient
water to make abstraction economic. It was calculated that firms
producing chemicals which employ less than approximately 190 persons
are unlikely to abstract water privately. As far as total supplies are
concerned the negative constant could be thought to indicate the
minimum size of the labour force in a viable chemical plant, but, as the
sample was deliberately biased towards firms employing over 15 persons,
it is not possible to draw any such inferences from the result.

A final variable which is significantly related to the quantity of water
*purchased* is the price paid to the local undertakings for each 1,000 gallons
of supply. Only firms receiving a metered water supply were included in
this section of the regression analysis; unmetered concerns were omitted
as they do not pay a price for each unit of water taken, and therefore price
changes will not influence their demands. Although the best-fit equation
form $\log Q = a + bP_m$ only produced an $R^2$ value of 0.11 (11%), this low
level of explanation was to be expected when no differentiation of firms
into size or type groups was made. As the established relationship between

price and quantity was a significant one, at the 0.95 level of probability, it was possible to calculate an approximate price elasticity[9] for the water demands of chemical plants. When the elasticity was calculated about the mean price of 31.75 pence per 1,000 gallons it proved to be just inelastic at a value of $-0.958$. However, when the price is increased by only 2d per 1,000 gallons the regression line becomes elastic. Therefore, at prices over approximately 34 pence per 1,000 gallons the quantity of water purchased by chemical manufacturers is more than proportionately responsive to price. As the best-fit equation form is $\log Q = a + bP_m$, it would appear that at high price levels the regression line becomes steeper, and this implies that very large increases in price would cause only small decreases in the quantity of water taken.[10] This suggests that chemical plants will purchase a minimum quantity of water even at very high prices in order to remain in business. On the other hand at low prices the regression curve becomes relatively flat, and large decreases in the quantity of water demanded would accompany small price rises.

The level of explanation ($R^2$) was significantly improved when the quantity of water abstracted privately by each chemical plant was included in the regression of quantity purchased on price. 33.9% of the variation between firms in the amount of water *purchased* was explained by the best-fit equation form which was $\log Q = a + b\log_i P + c\log QA$. In other words the inclusion of data on the level of private abstraction has partly differentiated between the different demand curves for purchased water of firms relying solely on bought supplies and those abstracting some water privately. Firms with their own sources of supply should have a more elastic demand curve for purchased water as to a certain extent they are able to substitute privately abstracted water for purchased water. This substitute is not available to firms without a private supply source.

It must be emphasized that although price *is* a significant explanatory variable of demand it is much less important than ton-input or employment in determining the level of water usage within the chemical industry. When tonnage of raw materials or the level of employment was added to a regression equation containing price as an explanatory variable, price became insignificant. In other words, if a firm increased the number of persons employed it would also increase its water consumption and price rises would not prevent this increase, although possibly the rate of increase in demand would be decreased. This feature is of considerable importance to water planning and control and will be considered in greater detail in Chapter 6.

**Table 11. Determinants of the quantity of water taken by food firms**

| dependent variable 1 | significant independent variables 2 | best-fit equation form 3 | regression coefficient (b) 4 | standard error 5 | 'T' test value (significance level) 6 | degrees of freedom 7 | level of explanation ($R^2$) 8 |
|---|---|---|---|---|---|---|---|
| A purchased water | raw materials: tonnage | $Q^2 = a + bT$ | 1516781173.02 | 30784595.73 | 24.28 | 15 | 86.7% |
| | employment | $Q = a + bE$ | 131.664 | 20.976 | 39.40 | 15 | 72.4 |
| | price of metered water | $\log Q = a + bP_m$ | −0.1312 | 0.0312 | 19.335 | 13 | 59.8 |
| B abstracted water | raw materials: tonnage | $QA^2 = a+bT$ | 756270094.8 | 93673051.9 | 65.18 | 15 | 90.7 |
| | employment | $QA^2 = a+bE$ | 143984583.0 | 36087327.9 | 15.92 | 15 | 51.5 |
| C total water taken | raw materials: tonnage | $Qt^2 = a+bT$ | 1550294615.9 | 54891162.05 | 797.67 | 15 | 99.4 |
| | employment | $Qt^2 = a+bE$ | 345720920.12 | 67704958.8 | 26.07 | 15 | 63.5 |
| D purchased water | abstracted water | $Q = a+bQA$ | 0.3379 | 0.0882 | 14.68 | 15 | 55.4 |

No multiple regression equation containing tonnage and employment was attempted due to multicollinearity.

D*

## 2 *Food production*

In many respects the regression results for the food sub-group were similar to those of the chemical industry. One important similarity that arose was that the tonnage of raw materials entering the manufacturing process proved to be the best explanatory variable of water usage (table 11). The best-fit regression equation forms were also alike for the two industry groups, although the levels of explanation derived from them were lower in the case of food production.

Tonnage of raw materials was positively related to the quantity of water *purchased* from local undertakings, the correlation being greatest when the equation $Q^2 = a + bT$ was used. It was calculated from the regression coefficients[11] that the slope of the regression line about the mean tonnage was 954.5 gallons per ton. In other words at this point on the curve an addition of 1,000 tons of raw materials is associated with an increase in the demand for purchased water of approximately 950,000 gallons per annum, although individual firms in the food industry will increase their water demands by a range of values around this gallonage.

The shape of the regression curve implies that marginal increments to the quantity of water purchased will decrease above the mean tonnage, and although the increments will remain positive the rate of increase will decline steadily as tonnage increases. As in the chemical industry it is probable that this declining rate of increase is due to the substitution of privately abstracted water for bought supplies when large gallonages of water are required. Below the mean tonnage demand for water will increase by more than 950,000 gallons per annum when 1,000 tons of raw materials are added.

Raw material usage was also the best independent variable when used to explain variations in both the level of *private abstraction,* and the quantity of water used *in total* by food producers. A squared equation form ($QA^2$ or $Qt^2 = a + bT$) yielded the highest $R^2$ value and the highest level of significance in both cases. Although the resultant regression lines were similar in shape to that for *purchased supplies*, it was found that the slopes were steeper. An addition of 1,000 tons of raw material inputs is associated with an increase of approximately 5.8 million gallons per annum in the quantity of *water abstracted*, and 2.5 million gallons per annum in the *total* demand for water.

One important difference between the regression results for the food and chemical industries emerged when the constant terms of the equations were studied. In the food group the constant term was negative in the equation relating ton-input to the quantity of water *purchased*, whereas in the chemical industry it was positive. There appear to be two possible explanations of the negative constant term. In the first instance it could suggest that there is a minimum economic size of food manufacturing plants. The minimum sized plant would take approximately 30,000 tons of raw materials a year (although there will be a range of values around the point where the regression line cuts the tonnage axis). A second possibility is that the regression line intersects the tonnage axis at a positive value because of the bias in the 'Industrial Survey' towards the larger firms. As there is a strong correlation between the number of persons employed and the quantity of raw materials used in the food industry it is possible that the exclusion of firms employing under 15 persons has resulted in the exclusion of firms using small quantities of raw materials. The negative constant may in fact have been produced by the combination of these two features.

Rather unexpectedly the constant regression coefficient in the equation relating tonnage of raw materials to the level of private abstraction undertaken by food producers was positive; in the chemical industry it was negative. Again the sign is capable of two explanations. Firstly it is possible that no food firm would consider private abstraction unless approximately 140 million gallons of water were required each year;[12] this minimum economic level would apply irrespective of the quantity of raw materials used by the firm. It is possible that the gallonage reflects the minimum economic size of water abstracting and cleaning equipment. On the other hand, the result may be another product of the sample bias towards larger plants, as figure 7 shows.

If there were no firms in the computations taking less than $O - T$ tons of raw materials then $a - b$ will be the fitted regression line, and this extrapolated to the quantity abstracted axis gives a positive constant $c$. However, if additional observations were available to the left of the line $T - T$, then the appropriate regression line may well have been $d - e$, which gives a negative constant term $f$. The value of tonnage at point $e$ would then have shown the minimum amount of raw materials which a food producer must use before sufficient water is needed to make private abstraction an economic proposition.

A second highly significant explanatory variable of the quantities of water purchased and abstracted by food manufacturers is the number of persons employed (see table 11). This variable, however, did not produce levels of explanation ($R^2$) as high as those given by ton-input. Employment is most important in explaining the variation between food firms in the quantity of water *purchased*; a linear equation $Q = a + bE$

**Figure 7  One possible effect of sample bias towards larger plants**

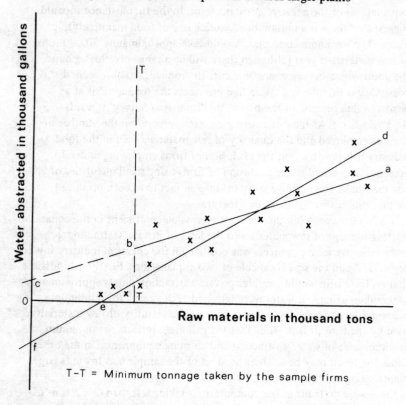

T–T = Minimum tonnage taken by the sample firms

accounted for 72.4% of the variation. Explanation levels are not so high for the regressions on *privately abstracted* or *total* water, being 51.5% and 63.5% respectively. As the water required for staff hygiene purposes is most commonly purchased from local water undertakings it is to be expected that bought supplies should be most closely correlated to employment.

As the relationship between the gallonage of water *purchased* and the number of persons employed is linear the slope of the regression line is constant. Uniform marginal increments of approximately 130,000 gpa[13] are associated with the addition of one employee. The relationship between employment and the level of *private abstraction* is best described mathematically by the equation $QA^2 = a + bE$. Calculated about the mean level of employment the slope of the established regression line was 670,000 gallons per annum for each additional employee, but the shape of the curve suggests that marginal increases in the quantity of water abstracted will decrease at the higher employment levels. Employment against the *total* quantity of water taken also produced the highest level of explanation when the equation $Qt^2 = a + bE$ was fitted. In this case the slope of the regression line (550,000 gpa per additional employee) was less steep than that for abstracted water, but steeper than that for purchased supplies.

Each equation in which the number of persons employed was used as the independent explanatory variable of water usage by food producers yielded a negative constant term. No water is purchased by firms employing less than 25 persons, and therefore it is implied that this is the minimum size for a viable food producing plant. It is, however, possible that this minimum figure arises from the already mentioned sample bias towards larger firms and plants. The negative constant term in the equation relating employment to the level of private abstraction suggests that firms employing less than 140 persons will not demand large enough gallonages of water to make private abstraction worthwhile. This minimum employment figure is only an approximation as there is a scatter of sample observations about the regression line.

The price paid per 1000 gallons for metered supplies of water is also a significant explanatory variable for purchased water. A logarithmically transformed equation ($\log Q = a + bP_m$) explained nearly 60% of the variation between food producers in the quantity of water purchased. As expected the relationship was negative, with demand for water decreasing as price increased. From the regression coefficient $b$ it was possible to calculate the price elasticity at various points on the demand curve for water. At all the observed prices the curve proved to be elastic; elasticity was 3.288 at the lowest recorded price and this increased to 6.713 for the highest recorded price, which was 49 pence per 1000 gallons. It was found that these results are significant at the 99.95 level of probability and therefore there is a strong case for concluding that food producers are highly responsive to the price of metered water supplies. However, it must be acknowledged that the elasticities may be inflated due to the 'identification problem'.[14]

## 3 Drink manufacturers

In many respects the results of the sample survey were most unsatisfactory for this industry sub-group. As has already been mentioned, it proved exceptionally difficult to obtain responses from the brewers, who make

Table 12. Determinants of the quantity of water taken by drink firms

| dependent variables 1 | significant independent variables 2 | best-fit equation form 3 | regression coefficient (b) 4 | standard error 5 | 'F' test value (significance level) 6 | degrees of freedom 7 | level of explanation ($R^2$) 8 |
|---|---|---|---|---|---|---|---|
| A purchased water | price of metered water | $Q = a + b \log P_m$ | −427400.0 | 230750.0 | 3.4308 | 6 | 36.28 * |
| B abstracted water | raw materials: tonnage | $\log QA = a + bT$ | −0.07914 | 0.02257 | 12.30 | 8 | 77.4 |

* This relationship was only significant at the 0.90 level of probability.

up a substantial proportion of the drink firms located in the south east. Large abstractors of private supplies of water were especially reluctant to divulge details about the quantity or quality of their requirements. Some of them suggested that such information would allow a competitor to work out the manufacturing process, and the mineral content of the beer. Whatever the reason for their reluctance to answer the industrial questionnaire the low reponse rate of 30% has affected the results in two main ways. First the number of observations and the resultant degrees of freedom in the regression are small, and this makes it difficult to establish significant explanatory relationships. Second, there is a marked bias in the sample towards the smaller drink producers, relying on bought water supplies, which means that the importance of water as an element in the cost structure of drink producers and as a location factor is probably grossly underestimated.

As table 12 shows only one regression equation, out of over 50 which were run, established a relationship which was significant at the 0.95 level of probability. The relationship was between the quantity of water *abstracted privately* and the tonnage of raw materials used in the manufacturing process, and the form $\log QA = a + bT$ explained 77.4% of the variation in the quantity of water abstracted by the observed firms. One important and unexpected feature of the relationship is that the regression coefficient $b$ is negative; in other words as ton-input increases the quantity of water abstracted declines. In fact the regression curve suggests that drink manufacturers which use over 90,000 tons of raw materials will not abstract any water privately. It is just possible that the negative correlation arises because some drink manufacturers use very small quantities of raw materials in relation to the gallonage of water taken because water makes up a substantial part by weight of the product. A more probable explanation, however, is that the negative coefficient arises from the lack of response to the 'Industrial Survey' questionnaire from private abstractors in the drink industry.

Although the price paid for metered water did not prove significantly correlated with the quantity of water *purchased* at the 0.95 level of probability, the negative relationship was significant at the 0.90 level.[15] On the strength of this correlation the price elasticity of the established regression line was calculated, although it must be acknowledged that the accuracy of the results are more suspect than those for the other sub-groups. The best-fit equation form proved to be $Q = a + b \log P_m$, which explained 36.3% of the variation in the quantity of water purchased by drink firms. Calculated about the mean gallonage the price elasticity of the regression line was 4.1, which is highly elastic. At the lowest recorded quantity of water purchased the elasticity was even higher, but at the largest recorded purchase the curve was only just elastic with a value of 1.3. The shape of the curve is thus the normal one for a demand curve with the elasticity being greatest when price is high and the quantity purchased is low.

## 4 *The paper and paper products industry*

When this industry group was treated as a whole the regression results were poor, with levels of explanation and significance below those obtained for many of the other industry groups. It was suspected that these low levels stemmed from the polyglot nature of the industry group, which contains raw paper manufacturers on the one hand, and firms assembling cardboard boxes on the other. Whereas most raw paper producers used over 10 mgy, it was usual for product manufacturers to take less than 500,000 gpy. Ideally two separate regression analyses should have been completed, one for the primary and one for the secondary stages of manufacture, but the degrees of freedom in the regression equation would have been decreased and it would have been difficult to obtain significant results. In view of this, it was decided to differentiate between the two distinct manufacturing types by adding a dummy variable to each best-fit equation form.[16] It was hoped that this would give markedly improved levels of significance and explanation, but in fact any improvements were marginal as table 13 shows.

The number of persons employed was the independent variable most significantly related to the quantity of water *purchased* by paper firms from their local undertakings. A simple linear equation produced the highest $R^2$ value of 0.2252 (22.5%), and employment and purchased water usage were significantly related at the 0.95 level of probability. As this is a linear equation the slope of the regression line is constant, with an increase of approximately 118,000 gallons a year per additional employee. This does not mean to say that the quantity of water purchased can be found by multiplying the number of persons employed by 118,000, because the regression constant is negative. In other words there is a minimum employment level for the firms surveyed in the paper group, and so the regression line crosses the employment axis at a positive value. This minimum figure is in part the result of the deliberate biasing of the sample towards larger plants,[17] but it does also represent a true minimum economic plant size. The latter factor is especially valid for raw paper producers, where the scale of equipment necessary for economic

**Table 13. Determinants of the quantity of water taken by paper and paper product firms**

| dependent variables 1 | significant independent variables 2 | best-fit equation form 3 | regression coefficient (b) 4 | standard error 5 | 'T' test value (significance level) 6 | degrees of freedom 7 | levels of explanation ($R^2$ values) without dummy 8a | with dummy 8b |
|---|---|---|---|---|---|---|---|---|
| **A** purchased water | employment | $Q = a + bE$ | 118.48 | 49.27 | 5.78 | 20 | 22.43% | 22.52% |
| | price of metered water | $\log Q = a + bP_m$ | −0.0601 | 0.0331 | 3.29 | 10 | 24.76* | 24.81* |
| | multiple regression { price of bought water, quantity of water abstracted } | $\log Q = a + b \log P + c \log QA$ | 1.9809 / 0.1843 | 0.4109 / 0.0861 | 23.24 / 4.59 | 19 | 55.3 | — |
| **B** privately abstracted water | Raw materials: tonnage | $QA = a + bT$ | 20109.96 | 3647.84 | 30.39 | 20 | 60.31 | 63.15 |
| | employment | $QA = a + bE$ | 1130.30 | 398.46 | 8.04 | 20 | 28.69 | 33.96 |
| | price of bought water | $\log QA = a + bP$ | −0.0891 | 0.02918 | 9.32 | 20 | 15.6 | 15.7 |
| **C** total water usage | employment | $\log Qt = a + bE$ | 0.00267 | 0.00077 | 12.13 | 20 | 37.8 | 39.3 |
| | raw materials: tonnage | $Qt = a + bT$ | 20004.13 | 3552.00 | 25.86 | 20 | 69.9 | 71.8 |
| | price of bought water | $\log Qt = a + bP$ | 0.04139 | 0.01401 | 8.73 | 20 | 11.7 | 11.8 |

* only significant at the 0.90 level of probability.

production sets an employment minimum of approximately 128 persons.

As Column 8b of table 13 shows, the addition of a dummy variable to the employment—quantity bought equation increases the level of explanation only marginally. It is possible that the fact that three of the raw paper producers do not purchase *any* water from the local authorities has lessened the value of the dummy. In addition it could be that raw paper firms substitute abstracted water for purchased supplies, which again would decrease the differences in the quantity of water *purchased* by the two manufacturing types.

When the price of metered water was regressed against the quantity of water *bought* the best-fit equation form $\log Q = a + bP_m$ produced an $R^2$ of 0.247 (25%). This result was not significant at the 0.95 level of probability, although the Students '$t$' test showed that there was a correlation at the 0.90 level. As expected the relationship established between price and quantity bought was a negative one, with purchases decreasing as price increased. When the elasticity of demand was calculated about three price values, the mean, the lowest recorded payment of 24 pence per 1000 gallons, and the highest of 48 pence, it was found that the curve was elastic along its whole length, although at the lowest price it was only just elastic. The shape of the regression line was an expected one with elasticity decreasing as price falls.

| | price | | elasticity |
|---|---|---|---|
| highest price | 48 | pence per 1000g. | 2.8848 |
| mean price | 32.5 | pence per 1000g. | 1.9532 |
| lowest price | 24 | pence per 1000g. | 1.4424 |

Once again the addition of a differentiating dummy variable to the equation failed to produce a significant increase in the level of explanation.

The quantity of water *abstracted* also served to differentiate between the different demand curves for *purchased* water exhibited by raw paper and paper product manufacturers. Only one of the surveyed product firms owned a private source of supply. An $R^2$ value of 0.553 (55%) was produced by a logarithmically transformed equation containing both the price paid for purchased water and the quantity of water abstracted; this is a large improvement over the level of explanation derived by using price alone as an explanatory variable. The result, however, does pose a difficult problem of interpretation, as the price coefficient is now positive. This suggests that firms take more water as the price increases, which is not only directly contradictory to the previous regression but is logically untenable. As the observations are widely scattered the inclusion of the quantity of water abstracted as a second explanatory variable was able to alter the slope of the regression line. The dummy variable was not added to the best-fit equation as the quantity of water abstracted itself acts to differentiate between the two manufacturing types.

A similar problem of an inappropriate sign also arose when the relationship between the *price of bought supplies* and the *quantity of water abstracted privately* was explored. At the 0.95 level of probability a significant relationship emerged when the equation $\log QA = a + bP$ was run, but the resultant regression coefficient was negative. In other words as the price of bought water increases the rate of abstraction decreases, whereas for there to be a price-cross effect the quantity of water abstracted should rise as the price of bought supplies increases. The apparently paradoxical result is probably partly caused by the omission from the regression equation of the pricing methods practised by the water undertakings in whose areas the firms are located. It was found that eight of the product firms are charged on rateable value for their supplies of purchased water,[18] and in addition none of them abstracted any water. This means that a high price for purchased water is linked with a zero level of private abstraction. Another reason for the lack of a price-cross effect is the fact that three of the raw paper producers each abstract 1400 mgy from private sources and do not purchase any water from the local undertakings. Therefore a zero price for purchased water is linked with a high level of private abstraction. As these eleven observations account for half of all the firms in this sub-group which supplied water consumption information, a negative regression coefficient was produced (see figure 8). The low level of explanation is probably caused by the wide scatter of the other observations around the regression line. When the dummy variable was added to the regression equation there was only a marginal increase in the $R^2$ value.

Due to the positive sign of the coefficient and the low $R^2$ value the price of bought water was only a poor independent variable explaining the level of *private abstraction*, but both the quantity of raw materials and the number of persons employed had much greater explanatory power. The tonnage of raw materials entering the manufacturing process explained 60.31% of the variation in the quantity of water obtained from private sources, when the equation form $QA = a + bT$ was used. As the equation is a normal linear one the slope of the regression line is constant, and an addition of 1000 tons of raw material input causes the quantity of water abstracted to increase by approximately 20 million gallons[19] a year. The regression equation produced a positive constant term which implies that approximately 200 million gallons per annum must be demanded

**Figure 8 The relationship between the price of bought water and the quantity abstracted privately by paper firms**

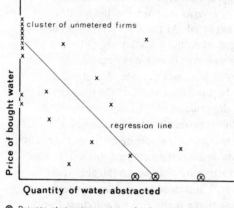

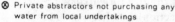

⊗ Private abstractors not purchasing any
water from local undertakings

before abstraction from a private source becomes worthwhile. Raw paper producers must have access to large quantities of cooling and process water before the manufacturing process is possible; these requirements are usually met from private abstraction as purchased water would not be economic. When a dummy variable was added to the best fit equation, an increase in explanation of almost 3% occurred giving an $R^2$ of 63.15%.

Employment proved to be most significantly related to the level of *private abstraction* when a normal linear equation was used; 28.7% of the variation was explained and this increased to 34% when a dummy variable was added. The slope of the regression line is positive and constant, with each additional employee being associated with an increase of 1.1 mgy in the quantity of water privately abstracted. It can be seen that the slope of this regression line is much steeper than that for the employment-bought water computation. From the value of the positive constant term $a$ it has been estimated that approximately 228 mgy must be taken before private abstraction is an economic proposition. This figure agrees relatively closely with that derived from the equation $QA = a + bT$.

When *total water usage* was taken as the dependent variable it was found that the results had many features in common with those for abstracted water. In the first place the price of bought water was

significantly but negatively related to total water usage. Secondly, the
tonnage of raw materials entering the manufacturing process was the
best explanatory variable, accounting for 70% of the variation in the
quantity of water taken in total. Thirdly the slope of the regression line
relating raw materials to total water usage was virtually the same as that
relating this independent variable to the level of private abstraction; each
additional 1000 tons of raw materials is associated with an increase of
20 mgy in total water demands. A final similarity is that the number
of persons employed was also a significant determinant of water usage.
The close coincidence of the two sets of results was expected as privately
abstracted supplies account for 99% of the total water used by the
respondent paper firms.

## 5 *Plastics and rubber manufacturing*
In this industrial sub-group the simple regression equations failed to
establish any significant relationships between the five independent
variables and the quantity of water taken. As the industry group is more
highly differentiated than the other sub-groups it is possible that simple
relationships are not powerful enough to isolate the various manufacturing
types. Ideally three separate regression analyses should have been run,
treating raw plastic producers, plastic product manufacturers and rubber
makers as distinct entities; unfortunately the sample frame does not allow
sub-groups to be formed to this level of disaggregation. An attempt to
circumvent this defect in the sample was made by devising multiple
regression models capable of isolating at least some of the different
manufacturing types. The results of the multiple regression analysis
are given on table 14.

The correlation matrix for the plastics sub-group did not reveal a high
degree of intercorrelation between the number of persons employed and
the tonnage of raw materials used. It was therefore, possible to include
both of these independent explanatory variables in one regression model,
without multicollinearity distorting the results.[20] It was hoped that
variations in the level of ton-input would serve to differentiate between
the different types of manufacturing process, and so allow employment to
emerge as a significant explanatory variable of water usage. In fact this
process did produce a significant result when both employment and
tonnage were used to explain the variation between plastics firms in the
quantity of water *purchased* from local undertakings. The best fit
regression equation $Q^2 = a + bE + cT$ produced an $R^2$ value of 0.415
(41.5%) and employment was significantly related to demand, although

Table 14. Determinants of the quantity of water taken by plastic and rubber firms

| dependent variable 1 | significant independent variables 2 | best-fit equation form 3 | regression coefficient (b) 4 | standard error 5 | 'f' test value (significance level) 6 | degrees of freedom 7 | level of explanation ($R^2$) 8 |
|---|---|---|---|---|---|---|---|
| A purchased water | multiple regression { employment raw material ton-input | $Q^2 = a + bE + cT$ | 665511.15 3070739.3 | 309995.75 2400645.4 | 4.61 1.64 | 9 | 41.5% |
| | multiple regression { price of bought water quantity of water abstracted | $Q^2 = a + bP + cQA$ | 6187186.77 −58.19447 | 2839770.5 1341.397 | 4.75 0.00 | 9 | 37.8 |

No simple regression equations produced significant results at the 0.95 or 0.90 levels of probability.

Table 15. Determinants of the quantity of water taken by metals and metal product firms

| dependent variables 1 | significant independent variables 2 | best-fit equation form 3 | regression coefficient (b) 4 | standard error 5 | 'f' test value (significance level) 6 | degrees of freedom 7 | level of explanation ($R^2$) 8 |
|---|---|---|---|---|---|---|---|
| A purchased water | employment | $Q = a + bE^2$ | 0.02796 | 0.0017 | 270.05 | 11 | 96.1% |
| B abstracted water | employment | $QA = a + bE$ | 2.54422 | 0.3636 | 48.96 | 11 | 81.7 |
| C total water taken | employment | $Qt = a + bE$ | 67.2903 | 9.2578 | 52.83 | 11 | 82.8 |
| D purchased water | abstracted water | $Q^2 = a + bQA$ | 4622070.18 | 11882.77 | 151299.4 | 11 | 99.7 |

Multiple regressions using tonnage and employment failed to increase the levels of significance and explanation.

tonnage was not. However, the same two variables failed to produce
significant results when regressed against both the quantity of water
abstracted privately, and the quantity taken in total.

In an attempt to relate the price of purchased supplies to the quantity
of *water purchased* a second multiple regression model was used. The
quantity of water abstracted privately was introduced as a second
explanatory variable, and it was hoped that this would act to isolate
those firms using private water supplies in processing, as their demand
curve for purchased supplies should be more elastic than that of firms
relying solely on the local water undertakings. When the equation
$Q^2 = a + bP + cQA$ was run the price of purchased water was significantly
related to demand, and the regression explained 37.8% of the variation
in the quantity of water bought by plastic and rubber firms.

### 6 Metal and metal product manufacture

The number of persons employed is very closely related to the quantity
of water used by producers of metals and metal products (see table 15).
It was by far the most important independent explanatory variable,
explaining 96% of the variation between plants in the quantity of water
*purchased*, and over 80% of the variation in both the level of *private
abstraction* and the gallonage of water *taken in total*. The $R^2$ value is
higher in the regression on purchased supplies of water due to the close
linkage between the hygiene requirements of the factory workers, and
the supplies of potable water needed. The equation which best described
the relationship between employment and water purchases was
$Q = a + bE^2$; the shape of this curve implies that at the higher levels of
employment the marginal increment in the quantity of water bought
increases rapidly. It was found that all the observed metal firms purchase
at least 570,000 gallons per annum from the local authorities. This
minimum gallonage may have arisen because firms employing under
15 persons were excluded from the sample, but it is also possible
that metal plants demanding a smaller quantity of water each year
would not be large enough to be economically viable concerns.

Linear equation forms produced the highest levels of explanation in
the regressions which related employment to the quantity of water
*abstracted privately* and to the gallonage of water used in *total* by firms.
The slope of the regression line was, however, much steeper in the case
of total supplies, being 67,000 gpa per additional employee, whereas for
abstracted supplies an extra worker was *associated* with an increase of
only 2,500 gpa. This slope variation is the result of the high proportion

of bought water in the total amount taken; very few of the metal firms sampled in south east England own a private water supply source. In other regions of the country, in which manufacturers of raw metals are more common, it is probable that the level of private abstraction would be greater and that the regression line would have a steeper slope. It was found from the regression coefficients that only the largest sampled metal producers require a sufficient gallonage of water to make private abstraction worthwhile. Usually the plants will employ over 214 persons before private abstraction will be considered.

The tonnage of raw materials entering the manufacturing process rather surprisingly failed to emerge as a significant variable explaining water usage. Before the computations were made it was thought that ton-input would be significant and that it would serve to isolate the various manufacturing processes; this did not prove to be the case. One probable reason for this is that heavy metal manufacture is not well represented in the south east and the total population of such firms was too small to warrant their inclusion as a separate industrial stratum, distinct from metal product manufacturers. When firms were randomly selected only one primary metal manufacturer, the Enfield Rolling Mills at Brimsdown on the river Lea, appeared in the sample; the other respondent firms buy in their metal ingots, chiefly from plants in the Midlands. As metal product manufacturers require only small gallonages of water for use in processing and for cooling, the greatest proportion of their water usage is for staff hygiene purposes. It has already been seen that ton-input is is most closely related to the quantity of water used in process or for cooling, while employment best explains the gallonages used for sanitation.

When regressions were run using the price of purchased water as an independent variable no significant results were obtained. Even when the data were transformed there was no significant relationship between the price and the quantity of water taken. Likewise the cost of abstraction failed to be related to the quantity of water abstracted privately.

*7 Non-metallic minerals and miscellaneous building materials*
In the analysis of the relationship between employment and the quantity of water *purchased* certain similarities emerged between the results for this group (see table 16) and those for metal firms, discussed in the previous section. Employment was the most significant variable and it accounted for a high proportion of the variation between firms in the quantity of water *purchased*. The $R^2$ value was, however, slightly

Table 16. Determinants of the quantity of water taken by non-metallic mineral firms

| dependent variables 1 | significant independent variables 2 | best-fit equation form 3 | regression coefficient (b) 4 | standard error 5 | 'F' test value (significance level) 6 | degrees of freedom 7 | level of explanation ($R^2$) 8 |
|---|---|---|---|---|---|---|---|
| A purchased water | employment | $Q = a + bE^2$ | 0.12629 | 0.02445 | 26.69 | 13 | 67.2% |
| | price of metered water | $Q = a + b \log P_m$ | −62176.719 | 27780.8 | 5.01 | 11 | 31.29 |
| B abstracted water | raw materials: tonnage | $\log QA = a + bT$ | 0.0061 | 0.0029 | 4.38 | 13 | 27.5 |
| C purchased water | abstracted water | $\log Q = a + b \log QA$ | −0.71086 | 0.2765 | 6.61 | 13 | 66.9 |

Multiple regression models including tonnage and employment failed to improve the levels of significance and explanation.

lower for the non-metallic group, being 0.672 (67.2%). In both industries best fit of the regression line to the observations was achieved by the equation $Q = a + bE^2$, which implies an increasing marginal increment in the quantity of water purchased as the number of persons employed increases. The slope of the regression curve when calculated about the mean level of employment was, however, less steep for the metal firms than for the non-metallic mineral concerns. An increase of one employee was associated with an increase of 24,000 gpa in the quantity of water purchased by metal firms, and with an increase of 35,000 gpa for non-metallic mineral plants. A final similarity between the two groups was that the regression constants were both positive; in other words the observed firms all take a minimum gallonage of water irrespective of the number of persons employed. This minimum is lower for non-metallic mineral firms than it was for metal producers, being 150,000 gpa. There will, however, be a range of values around this figure, as all the observations are not on the regression line.

A second variable which was significantly related to the quantity of water purchased was the price paid for each 1000 gallons of metered supply. The best fit equation form $Q = a + b \log P_m$ explained 31.29% of the variation between non-metallic mineral firms in the gallonages taken from local water undertakings. As is the case for many of the other industrial sub-groups, the elasticity of the regression line (demand curve) is greater than unity for this group at all the observed price levels. At the lowest price and the greatest quantity the elasticity equals 2.5, and this increases as price rises.

When the dependent variable was the quantity of water taken from *private sources* the only independent variable to achieve significance at the 0.95 level of probability was the tonnage of raw materials entering the manufacturing process. From the shape of the best-fit regression equation $\log QA = a + bT$ it would appear that the marginal increment in the quantity of water abstracted privately increases rapidly as the level of ton-input rises. A wide scatter of observations occurs around the regression line as the level of explanation is low at 27.5%; the derived results are therefore unsuitable for use in forecasting.

When the *total quantity* of water taken was used as the dependent variable none of the simple or multiple regressions produced significant results.

As no intercorrelation emerged between the number of employees and the tonnage of raw materials within this group it was possible to use both independent variables in multiple regression models. It was found, however, that these models achieved no appreciable increases in either the level of explanation or the degree of significance.

## 8 *Mechanical and precision engineering*

As table 17 clearly shows, the results for the engineering sub-group were unsatisfactory; most of the independent variables were not significantly related to the quantities of water bought, abstracted or used in total.

When the price paid for water was used as the sole independent explanatory variable it was not significantly related to the quantity of water *purchased*. Significance did result, however, when the quantity of water abstracted was added to the regression equation as a second explanatory variable. An equation $\log Q = a + b \log P + c \log QA$ explained 44.1% of the variation between engineering firms in the quantity of water bought. The regression coefficient $b$ for price is positive, however, which implies that more water is purchased as price rises. It is unlikely that the relationship between price and quantity is a meaningful one and the regression line is not a demand curve for water. The inclusion of a second independent variable has probably altered the slope of the regression line between the highly scattered observations.

Employment figures were also not related to the quantity of water purchased from local water undertakings by engineering firms. This result was unexpected as all the other labour-intensive groups did show a strong correlation between the two variables due to the close linkage between staff hygiene requirements and water purchases. The number of persons employed was, however, *just* significant at the 0.95 level when regressed against both the quantity of water abstracted, and that taken in total. In both cases a 'cubed' equation form $QA^3$ (or $Qt^3$) $= a + bE$ produced the best-fit result. These equations have very little explanatory power; the $R^2$ values are below 15% and there is a wide scatter of observations about the fitted line. This curve may take a number of forms but in this case it would appear to be approximately as shown in figure 9. The constant term for the equation $QA^3 = a + bE$ is negative and this implies that only firms employing over 400 persons will locate to and abstract from a private water source. In the regression of employment on the total quantity of water used the constant term is also negative, but in this case the threshold value of employment is smaller. It would appear that only engineering firms employing over 140 persons completed the quantity questions in the 'Industrial Survey'; the effect of sample bias towards the larger firms is apparent in this industry group.

**Table 17. Determinants of the quantity of water taken by engineering firms**

| dependent variable 1 | significant independent variables 2 | best-fit equation form 3 | regression coefficient (b) 4 | standard error 5 | 't' test value (significance level) 6 | degrees of freedom 7 | level of explanation ($R^2$) 8 |
|---|---|---|---|---|---|---|---|
| | | | | | | | % |
| A purchased water | multiple regression { price of bought water + quantity of abstracted water } | $\log Q = a + b \log P + c \log QA$ | 1.2235 <br> -0.0910 | 0.5852 <br> 0.1310 | 4.37 <br> 0.42 | 10 | 44.1 |
| B abstracted water | employment | $QA^3 = a + bE$ | 596851306118.7 | 310565932262.0 | 3.69 | 11 | 25.1 |
| C total water taken | employment | $Qt^3 = a + bE$ | 607856505706.1 | 316195324127.3 | 3.70 | 11 | 25.1 |

Multiple regression equations using tonnage and employment failed to produce significant results.

**Figure 9 Graph of $QA^3$ (or $Qt^3$) = - $a$ + $bE$**

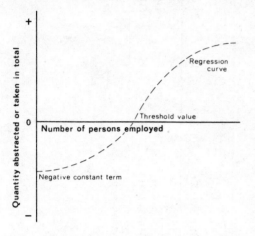

## 9 'Other' types of manufacture

A final group of firms which will be analysed in detail is a combination of clothing, textile, leather, fur, furniture, timber and printing firms. It was not possible to treat each of these manufacturing types as distinct industry groups as the number of available observations was too small to produce sufficient degrees of freedom within the regression equations. The low number of observations was not primarily due to the lack of response to the 'Industrial Survey' from firms in these industries; the printing group for example had an 80% response rate, and 70% of firms in the leather group replied to the questionnaire. Many of the respondent firms, however, did not complete the quantity questions on the survey form. Water is usually a minor or a completely unimportant factor in the locational and financial decisions of these firms and rarely do they use large quantities of the resource.

It proved possible to isolate some of the determinants of the quantity of water *purchased* by firms in this composite group, but none of the independent variables were significantly related to either the quantity of water *abstracted privately* or *used in total*. The actual manufacturing process in part determines whether private abstraction will take place; for example, it was found that textile producers and raw leather manufacturers frequently abstract water for cleaning, processing and dyeing. As in most other industry groups there is also the more random element of whether an abstraction site is available or not.

**Table 18. Determinants of the quantity of water taken by 'other' firms**

| dependent variables 1 | significant independent variables 2 | best-fit equation form 3 | regression coefficient $b$ 4 | standard error 5 | 'F' test value (significance level) 6 | degrees of freedom 7 | level of explanation ($R^2$) 8 |
|---|---|---|---|---|---|---|---|
| A purchased water | employment | $Q = a + bE^2$ | 0.0147 | 0.0018 | 67.06 | 14 | 87.02 % |
| | raw materials: tonnage | $Q = a + bT$ | 71.136 | 12.385 | 32.987 | 14 | 76.74 |
| | multiple regression $\{$ employment + price of bought water | $\log Q = a + bE + cP$ | 0.0034 | 0.0007 | 23.433 | 13 | 76 |
| | | | −0.0164 | 0.0042 | 14.964 | | |

No multiple regression model containing employment and tonnage was run due to multicollinearity.

The number of persons employed emerged as the best explanatory variable of the variation between firms in the quantity of water *purchased* from local water undertakings; an equation form $Q = a + bE^2$ had an $R^2$ value of 0.87 (87%). This type of equation implies that the regression line becomes progressively steeper as higher levels of employment are reached. In other words larger firms take proportionately more water than smaller ones. One possible reason for this is that larger firms may well take more water for processing and boiler-feed purposes. About the mean employment figure of 181 workers the slope of the regression line is 0.651 thousand gallons per head per annum, or in other words at this point one additional employee is associated with an increase of 650 gallons per annum in the quantity of water purchased. It is not correct to infer from this low gallonage that only approximately 3 gallons per employee are used for staff hygiene each working day. The regression constant of the equation is positive and therefore each manufacturer takes a minimum gallonage of water irrespective of the number of persons employed. In this composite group the minimum level of water purchases is approximately 90,000 gallons per annum, although there is a scatter of values around this figure. Part of the minimum gallonage goes to increase the daily usage of water for sanitation and hygiene by each employee.

A second explanatory variable that was significantly related to the quantity of water purchased from local undertakings was the tonnage of raw materials entering the manufacturing process. A simple linear equation $Q = a + bT$ explained 76.74% of the variation in the quantity of water bought by the respondent firms in this industry group. As the equation is linear, the slope of the regression line is constant; and addition of 1000 tons of raw materials is associated with an increase of 71,000 gallons per annum in the quantity of water purchased. The constant term of the regression is positive as it was in the equation using employment as the independent variable. This implies that all concerns will purchase over a minimum or threshold quantity of water whenever manufacturing occurs, irrespective of the tonnage of raw materials used. From the equation $Q = a + bT$ it would appear that all firms purchase over 87,000 gpa, which agrees well with the figure of 90,000 gpa given by the equation $Q = a + bE^2$. Tonnage of raw materials used was strongly correlated with the number of persons employed, therefore the two variables could not be used in one multiple regression model, as the results would be distorted by multicollinearity.

When the price paid for each 1000 gallons of water was used as the sole independent variable in a simple regression model no significant relationship could be established between the price paid and the quantity purchased. The lack of correlation arose because only four of the respondent firms are provided with a metered supply of water. Unmetered firms do not pay a unit price for their supplies and therefore they cannot be responsive to price changes. On the other hand, in those industry groups in which most of the firms were supplied on a meter the price elasticity of the demand curve was greater than one, and therefore the firms are responsive to price changes.

Price only became significantly related to the quantity of water purchased by firms in the 'other' group, when the variable was included in a multiple regression model. The model which related the logarithmically transformed quantity purchased to employment and price ($\log Q = a + bE + cP$) explained 76% of the variation between firms in the quantity of water purchased; 31% of the explanation was accounted for by the price variable. It is, however, doubtful whether this relationship is a demand function even though the sign of the relationship is negative. In all probability the correlation stems from the fact that many of the small concerns are charged on rateable value. These firms, therefore, pay a higher price per 1,000 gallons, and because they have few employees they take small gallonages of water. On the other hand the metered firms are normally larger, and demand greater quantity of water, but the price paid per 1000 gallons is lower.

## Summary

Much of the discussion in this chapter is summarized in table 19 which shows the equations which best explain the variation between firms in the quantity of water taken from private and public sources of supply. In other words it isolates the probable major determinants of industrial water consumption.

Levels of explanation and degrees of significance were much higher when firms were analysed by industry group than when all firms were treated together. For example, only 35% of the variation between all firms was explained by a multiple regression equation $\log Q = a + b \log E + c \log I + 1\ d \log P$, whereas in some of the sub-groups over 80% of the variation was accounted for by simple regression equations. This reflects the fact that the type of manufacturing process is an important independent variable explaining the quantity of industrial water taken; the 'industrial structure' of a region will partly determine the level of industrial water usage. In addition the uses to which water is put, and the sources from which demand is satisfied also varies greatly between industry groups.

E

**Table 19. Comparison of the best-fit explanatory equations in the industry groups**

| industry group | purchased water | | privately abstracted water | | total water taken | |
|---|---|---|---|---|---|---|
| | best-fit explanatory equation | level of explanation ($R^2$) | best-fit explanatory equation | level of explanation ($R^2$) | best-fit explanatory equation | level of explanation ($R^2$) |
| 1 | 2 | 3 | 4 | 5 | 6 | 7 |
| | | % | | | | |
| A chemicals | $Q^2 = a + bT$ | 97.2 | $QA = a + bT*$ | 100 | $Qt = a + bT*$ | 100 |
| B food | $Q^2 = a + bT$ | 86.7 | $QA^2 = a + bT$ | 90.7 | $Qt^2 = a + bT$ | 99.4 |
| C drink | $Q = a + b \log P_m$ | 36.3 | $\log QA = a + bT$ | 77.4 | NS | – |
| D plastics and rubber | $Q^2 = a + bE + cT$ | 41.5 | NS | – | NS | – |
| E paper and products | $\log Q = a + b \log P + c \log QA$ | 55.3 | $QA = a + bT$ | 60.31 | $Qt = a + bT$ | 91.8 |
| F non-metallic minerals | $Q = a + bE^2$ | 67.2 | $\log QA = a + bT$ | 27.5 | NS | – |
| G metals and products | $Q = a + bE^2$ | 96.1 | $QA = a + bE$ | 81.7 | $Qt = a + bE$ | 82.8 |
| H engineering (precision plus mechanical) | $\log Q = a + b \log P + c \log QA$ | 44.1 | $QA^3 = a + bE$ | 25.1 | $Qt^3 = a + bE$ | 25.1 |
| I other (leather and fur, clothing and textiles, timber and furniture, printing) | $Q^2 = a + bE$ | 87 | NS | | NS | – |
| total | $\log Q = a + b \log E + c \log T + d \log P$ | 34.9 | $\log QA = a + b \log P + c \log E + d \log T + c \log C$ | 16.6 | $\log Qt = a + b \log E + c \log T + d \log P$ | 47.3 |

* The equations $QA^2$ $(Qt)^2 = a + bT$ also produced an $R^2$ of 100% in this group.
NS: No equation achieved significance at the 0.95 or 0.90 levels of probability.

Two variables, tonnage of raw materials and the number of persons employed, were most closely related to water usage in virtually all the industry groups. The tonnage of raw material inputs produced very high levels of explanation when regressed against the water purchases, the level of private abstraction and total water usage of plants in the food and chemical industries. It also best explains the variation in the quantity of water abstracted privately by manufacturers of paper, drinks and non-metallic minerals. Employment was the most successful explanatory variable of the quantity of water purchased by metal manufacturers, non-metallic mineral producers and 'other' firms. It would appear that the amount of raw materials used by plants best explains water consumption in those industries in which water enters the manufacturing process or is used for cooling. On the other hand, employment produces higher levels of significance and explanation when most of the water is used for staff hygiene purposes.

Although most of the industrial sub-groups appear to have demand curves for bought water which are price elastic, price is rarely the most significant explanatory variable of the quantity of water purchased. The only exception to this statement occurs in the drink group where price was most closely related to demand. In two of the industry groups, paper and engineering, price only became significant at the 0.95 level of probability when the quantity of water abstracted was included in the regression model; in both cases problems of interpretation arose due to the positive sign of the coefficient $b$.

It was found that the length of time a firm has been located on its present site is not significantly related to the quantity of water demanded by firms in any of the industry groups. In the previous chapter it was also seen that no relationship was discovered between the age of the plant and water usage when all firms were included in one computation. Firms probably make internal changes to their water using equipment or staff hygiene facilities without completely rebuilding their premises, and therefore, any increase in consumption over time does not become apparent.

The final independent variable to be used in the explanation of the demand for water was the cost of private abstraction, and this also failed to emerge as a significant variable in any of the regressions. Amounts of water taken by abstraction from a private source of supply seem to be determined by the quantity requirements of the firm, and the capacity of the source rather than by cost considerations. In the future, however, the new licencing charges may well make cost a more important factor in determining the level of private abstraction.

# Chapter 5

# Water demand and industrial location

**Introduction**

In the two preceding chapters the factors which appear to influence the demand for water by manufacturing industry were discussed in some detail. Variations in these factors were used to explain the differences between firms in the quantity of water taken and in the sources from which the demand is satisfied. The influence of the demand for water of suitable quantity and quality on industrial location will now be considered.

Opinions on the role of water as a location factor have expressed a wide variety of often conflicting views. On the one hand some writers consider that water is a vital location factor, which is increasing in importance over time. For example, a paper presented by the United States Geological Survey maintains that,

. . . the location of industrial plants is dependent on an ample water supply of suitable quality. (130)

while in the United Nations publication *Water for Industrial Use* it is stated that,

Water supply is gaining in importance as a location factor and is playing a decisive role in the location of an increasing number of new or expanding industries and even in the relocation of existing ones. (128 p 2).

Although such views are most commonly found in American literature, some workers in Britain have made similar statements. Balchin, for example, says that,

Availability of water will increasingly control the location of industry in the future (6 p 477),

while Hopthrow suggests that in Britain,

Planning legislation and industrial expansion have imposed such substantial restrictions on the number of potential sites that today the availability of an abundant supply of water of the right quality may often be the dominant factor (i.e. in plant location)(54 p 30).

Such views as these are not universally accepted, however. Gilbert White, for example, has claimed that,

It may be argued from available evidence that the physical supply of water has not been a major factor in the location of industry in the United States and in several other industrial countries during recent years . . . (135).

Other writers, such as Sporck in his studies of industrial location in Belgium, have reached similar conclusions (107).

Traditionally location theorists have regarded water as a 'ubiquitous material', which 'is obtainable nearly everywhere, at costs so nearly the same that it does not enter the producers' transfer-cost reckoning at all' (53 p 35). By implication water is not regarded as a significant location factor and has accordingly been neglected in the literature on location theory.

Most of the views expressed on water's importance as a location factor in Britain are subjective as very little previous research has been undertaken on the topic; the lack of statistical evidence may well explain the variety of often conflicting views which are found. All opinions on the subject should be refuted or supported by empirical testing, and much of this chapter will be concerned with examining the influence of water supply on industrial location in south east England. Before beginning this examination, however, it is necessary to look briefly at the aims of location theorists as they have a direct bearing on the interpretation of the role of water as a location factor.

### Spatial and behavioural location theories

A distinction must be made between location theories which are designed to explain the regional distribution of economic activities and those which explain business locational decisions. Throughout the following discussion it is proposed to use the terms *spatial* or *macro* locational models for those theories which are concerned with spatial distributions, and the terms *behavioural* or *micro* models for those which deal with the decision making process.

It has been usual for theorists to attempt to explain how a firm reaches the decision to locate on a particular site as well as to describe and explain patterns of industrial distribution and differential regional growth rates. As McMillan has said,

. . . a frequent exercise of individuals and research organizations concerned with regional economics and more particularly regional industrial growth has been surveys of area manufacturers to determine why they chose a particular location (87 p 239).

The assumption has usually been made that an understanding of business location behaviour will lead to an understanding of regional growth and *vice versa*. But the two are not necessarily directly related, and factors which determine regional growth or stagnation need not be those considered important by individual business managers when making their locational decisions. If it is accepted that these two sets of factors are independent there are important implications for the interpretation of water as a location factor; its role will depend on whether *macro* or *micro* studies are being made.

There are in fact a number of reasons for the belief that regional location factors will not be considered in the locational decisions of individual factory managers. Firstly, regional industrial patterns are determined by *all* those factors which promote *success* in manufacturing. To a certain extent industrial success may result from a locational cost or sales advantage (such as nearness to a cheap raw material source) but other factors, including the amount and type of capital investment, varying managerial skills, varying research expenditure, and the products produced, are also vital considerations. These additional success factors will not contribute to the locational decisions of individual firms. Secondly, it is thought that the major component of regional growth is indigenous. When a region has a locational advantage for a particular type of manufacturing, firms are not normally drawn in from outside by the positive attraction of decreased costs or increased sales. Manufacturers already situated in the advantageous areas, however, are able to grow faster than similar producers located elsewhere. Growing firms will tend to extend output of existing products and will also tend to undertake experimentation and product diversification, which should lead to further success. Finally, it would seem likely that siting factors are the chief consideration when a manager is faced with the need to establish a branch plant or relocate a parent factory. It is relatively rare for the decision-maker to attempt to evaluate the comparative advantages and disadvantages of various regions.[1] In general the region is given and is the one in which the firm is already located or, in the case of an entirely new concern, with which the entrepreneur is familiar. Clearly siting factors are not regional growth factors.

The basis for the assertion that siting factors are the chief ones determining the actual decisions of factory managers is a simple behavioural model of industrial location. An outline of this will be given here briefly in order to be able to discuss the role of water supply as a factor in such a behavioural approach.[2]

## 1 *A micro-locational model*

Behavioural theorists, such as Cyert, Simon and March, view a firm as a collection of sectional interests, the aims of which may conflict. For example, shareholders presumably want increasing profits, managers desire increased salaries and status, while the labour force aims to increase wages, improve working conditions and to obtain shorter hours. Economists have used this idea of intra-firm conflict to explain the final pricing, output and profits policies of businesses, but the effect of conflict on industrial location and growth has not been examined. It is suggested here, however, that growth is the best way for a firm to resolve conflict, because as the firm expands profits, salaries and wages *can* all increase. Therefore, an important business aim is likely to be growth which may be induced by stimulating demand for the firm's output by advertising and product diversification. Firms will attempt, however, to expand at as little cost as possible in order to satisfy the shareholders demands for the level of distributed profits to be maintained during the period of costly physical expansion.

The idea of least-cost expansion has a number of implications for the way in which firms will behave when they are growing. It is likely that the demand for growth will first be satisfied by using existing equipment to capacity and by installing additional capital equipment within an existing plant. Further growth will probably take the form of on-site extensions to existing factory buildings (82 p 39). When all further possibilities of on-site expansion have been exhausted the businessman has to decide whether to increase capacity by buying up existing factories, merging with firms with spare capacity, or by seeking a new location for a branch or parent plant. The first two methods of growth are less costly than expansion on green-field sites (133) and therefore only rarely will a firm consider the question of looking for a new location. If a business manager is faced with the necessity of developing on a green-field site, he will still attempt to minimize the cost (including the cost in terms of effort and disruption). For this reason managers will normally begin their search for a new location within the area with which they are familiar; this is normally the area adjacent to the present factory or manager's home. The region of search is, therefore, usually given and the major managerial consideration is to find a *suitable* location in this area; siting factors determine what constitutes a suitable location. Such siting factors will include the availability of land, or a suitable building, the provision of adequate water and effluent disposal facilities, the availability of transport facilities on to the site, and the existence of a suitable labour supply in close proximity to the chosen location.

## 2 *The role of water in spatial theories of location*

At the present time a location theorist, aiming to produce a purely spatial theory, is probably justified in regarding water supply and effluent disposal facilities as minor factors, or in assuming ubiquity. In Britain it is highly unlikely that the development of, for example, the north east region *vis-à-vis* the south east has been affected by the supply of water, or that the inter-regional distribution of different types of manufacturing has been influenced by the availability of this resource. However, in the future it *may* become necessary to re-evaluate the importance of water as a factor in spatial location theories. Langdon White has pointed out that

. . . geographers were justified in regarding water as a minor factor in the past when the nations population was small, large cities were few and industrial development was relatively restricted but in the future increasing water shortage problems will cause the resource to affect regional industrial growth (136 p 463).

In the south east cases where industrial development has been affected, at least in the short-run, by pronounced water shortages have already arisen. For example, in December 1965 restrictions were placed on the number of houses built in Essex, and it was also reported that planning permission would be refused to industrial applicants using water heavily. (27.) These restrictions will only affect growth until 1971 when an extension to the developed water supplies will be completed. Similarly, in the Bishop's Stortford area of Hertfordshire, restrictions have been placed on house and factory building until new sewage disposal facilities are constructed on the Lea and its tributaries to combat the shortage of water to dilute effluent.[3] But if the present policy of providing developed water supplies to meet all foreseeable requirements is followed water shortages can have no long term influence on inter-regional growth, although the possibility remains that differential water prices could do so. However, as water costs are usually a very small proportion (under 1%) of total cost, it is unlikely that any effects on regional growth will be great. At very high water prices it would pay firms to install recycling and storage facilities, if the advantages for growth were very great in an area.

There is some evidence that the *intra*-regional industrial distribution may be influenced by the availability of plentiful water supplies. Previously, in Chapter 3 it was suggested that firms requiring water in quantities greater than that economically obtained from local water undertakings tend to locate to suitable abstraction sources. This encourages the concentration of large water using industries, such as paper, chemicals and non-metallic minerals, along water courses and above water bearing strata, which are in close proximity to urban areas.

## 3 *The role of water in bahavioural theories of location*
Whereas spatial patterns may not be influenced by water prices and availability, it cannot be assumed that these factors will not be considered by business managers when they make a locational decision. In fact as one of the siting factors water may play an important role in a behavioural theory of location. The rest of this chapter will be concerned with investigating the place of water *vis-à-vis* the other location factors in the decisions of firms. The variation in the importance of the resource between firms in different industry, size and age groups will also be considered. Finally, an attempt will be made to establish which internal characteristics of the firms are responsible for the varying importance of water within industry groups.

## a Information source
All the statistical data used in this section have been obtained from the 'Industrial Survey'. Each sampled firm was requested to rank the location factors in their order of importance to their decision to establish the factory on the present site (see Appendix B, question 2).The firms were also asked to consider the relative importance of each of the factors if they were to relocate the plant at the present time. The second set of rankings was requested for two reasons. Firstly, it was hoped that it would be possible to see whether factors had changed in importance over time. And secondly the hypothetical relocation rankings are comparable between firms as they were all considering conditions prevailing in 1966. The past rankings, on the other hand, may not be strictly comparable as each firm made the actual decision to locate on the present site in different years and may therefore have been influenced by particular conditions prevailing at that time.

It is recognised that ex-post subjective opinions about the importance

E*

of the locational factors are subject to considerable errors. Firms may
well rationalize what was essentially an irrational decision. In some firms
the men responsible for making the initial decision may no longer be
with the company and so their successors may guess the possible reasons
for the location. It is possible that some industrialists may have ranked
highest those factors traditionally thought to be important; this will tend
to deflate the rank given to water. Conversely the fact that the
questionnaire was concerned with water supply may have led the
manufacturer to inflate the true importance of the resource in his case.
While recognising all these as possible sources of bias, it is hoped that in
a random sample the errors will be distributed normally about the mean
zero, and will therefore tend to cancel each other out. An attempt to
evaluate and then eliminate some of the error was made by interviewing
a selected sample of the respondents, and discussing the true implication
of their replies.

b The results: the total position
From the rankings given by all the respondent firms, two frequency
distributions were calculated for each location factor. The first showed
the frequency with which factory managers placed the location factor in
ranks 1 to 8 when making the original decisions to locate on their present
sites. The second showed the distribution of ranks when the hypothetical
relocation decision was considered. Table 20 gives the results of these
tabulations.

In the past locational decision the factor which was ranked first with
the highest frequency was land; 37.6% of firms placed it first and a
further 21.5% placed it second. The same factor also emerged as most
important in the hypothetical relocation decision. These results lend
weight to the view discussed earlier that the most important element
in a firm's locational decision is the search for a suitable site, rather than
the comparative evaluation of various areas from the point of view of
profit advantage. The land factor was made to include both the availability
of sufficient land for expansion, and the existence of suitable buildings.

The market factor emerged with the second highest percentage of
ranks 1 and 2 in the actual past decision, but it was the third most
important factor in the relocation decision. At first sight the fact that
the market factor is given prominence in the location decisions of many
firms suggests that managers have considered the importance of the large,
high value market for their products in the south east and have therefore
located towards it. An alternative interpretation, however, was suggested

**Table 20. Proportion of firms ranking factors in order of their locational importance**
**Past Decision**

| factor | rank 1 | rank 2 | rank 3 | rank 4 | rank 5 | rank 6 | rank 7 | rank 8 |
|---|---|---|---|---|---|---|---|---|
| | % | % | % | % | % | % | % | % |
| A land | 37.6 | 21.5 | 16.9 | 9.1 | 5.8 | 1.2 | .4 | 7.4 |
| B market | 17.8 | 21.5 | 16.5 | 13.2 | 13.2 | 5.0 | 2.1 | 10.7 |
| c accident | 15.7 | 2.9 | 2.9 | 2.1 | 1.2 | 7.0 | 20.2 | 47.9 |
| D labour | 12.0 | 26.4 | 17.4 | 19.8 | 10.7 | 5.0 | 2.1 | 6.6 |
| E other | 6.6 | 2.9 | 1.7 | 1.2 | 1.7 | 3.3 | 25.2 | 57.4 |
| F raw material | 4.6 | 6.6 | 14.5 | 14.9 | 26.4 | 13.2 | 2.1 | 15.3 |
| G water supply | 4.1 | 5.4 | 7.4 | 6.6 | 5.0 | 28.9 | 21.1 | 22.8 |
| H transport | 3.7 | 8.7 | 14.0 | 21.1 | 20.6 | 16.1 | 2.5 | 13.2 |

**Hypothetical relocation decision**

| factor | rank 1 | rank 2 | rank 3 | rank 4 | rank 5 | rank 6 | rank 7 | rank 8 |
|---|---|---|---|---|---|---|---|---|
| A land | 36.0 | 25.2 | 18.2 | 12.0 | 5.8 | 1.7 | – | 1.2 |
| B labour | 29.3 | 27.7 | 17.4 | 12.0 | 9.9 | 2.9 | .8 | – |
| C market | 21.1 | 16.5 | 18.2 | 19.0 | 12.4 | 5.8 | 1.7 | 5.4 |
| D raw material | 4.6 | 6.6 | 15.3 | 17.8 | 30.6 | 13.6 | 1.7 | 7.8 |
| E water supply | 4.5 | 5.8 | 7.4 | 10.7 | 6.2 | 36.0 | 12.0 | 18.6 |
| F transport | 3.7 | 12.0 | 19.0 | 21.1 | 22.7 | 13.6 | 1.2 | 6.2 |
| G other | 3.3 | 2.1 | 1.7 | .8 | 1.7 | 5.8 | 40.5 | 44.2 |
| H accident | 1.2 | 1.7 | 1.2 | .8 | 1.2 | 5.0 | 23.6 | 65.3 |

at the interviews with the test firms. The majority of firms were not newly formed when they located on their present sites; they were therefore more concerned with remaining in contact with already established market outlets, rather than being positively attracted by the potential of the London market. The uncertainty of establishing new and reliable contacts outside the known area is one important force encouraging firms to relocate near their original or parent sites.

A third factor to emerge with a large number of high rankings in the past locational decision was 'accident', although it was not of importance in the relocation decision. This factor was made to include such elements as founders' birth-place or the buying up of an established firm. From the *behavioural* location model discussed earlier it was expected that the 'accident' factor would achieve importance in the actual siting decisions as entrepreneurs commonly establish new firms in the area with which they are familiar, and as many firms respond to increases in the demand for their product by purchasing existing plants with spare productive capacity. The fact that 'accident' is ranked highly suggests that only a relatively small number of firms have rationalized irrational or 'accidental' locations, and therefore confidence in the results is increased.

It would appear that the availability of a suitable labour force has increased in importance relative to the other location factors over time. In the past decision labour was ranked first by only 12% of firms, but this increased to 29.3% in the hypothetical relocation decision. The increasing importance may well reflect the tightening labour market in the south east.

All the remaining factors, raw materials, transport facilities, water supply and 'other'[4] were only placed first by approximately 5% of firms, this applies equally to both the past and present decisions. It was found that the range in the proportions was not great enough for them to be significantly different at the 0.95 level of probability. In other words it is not possible to say with any degree of confidence that any one of these remaining factors is more important than the others in the locational decisions of manufacturers in south east England.

Water is clearly not a critical consideration for the majority of firms when they are looking for a suitable site. It is, however, interesting to note that as few firms gave high ranks to the transport factor and to the availability of raw materials, two factors which have been prominent in traditional location theories. This result agrees with the findings of Twyman in his study of industry in east Kent (115). In all, 9.5% of the respondent firms regarded water as the first or second factor in their actual location decision, and 10.3% claimed that the resource would be the first or second consideration if relocation took place today. A further 7.4% of firms placed water as the third most important factor in both the past and present decisions. The very small percentage change over time in the number of firms ranking water highly is not sufficient to conclude that the resource is significantly increasing its importance over the years. There is no evidence that scarcity of available water supplies has caused firms to re-evaluate its position as a location factor. This point will be treated in more detail when the firms are sub-divided into age groups, based on the length of time they have occupied their present sites.

As 17% of the respondent firms gave water a high rank (1, 2 or 3), the suggestion is that for these firms the quantity or quality of available supplies, or the ease of effluent disposal were vital elements in their search for a suitable site. When the answers to question 10, Section B on the 'Industrial Survey' questionnaire (reproduced as Appendix B), were tabulated it was found that a similar proportion of firms (15.7%)

stated that the *quantity* of water required was a crucial consideration
in their locational decision (Table 21).

Table 21. The position of water quantity in a firm's locational decision

| position in locational decision | as a % of *all* respondent firms | As a % of firms completing the entire questionnaire | absolute numbers |
|---|---|---|---|
| crucial | 15.7% | 23.6% | 40 |
| important | 15.3% | 23.0% | 39 |
| minor | 16.1% | 24.2% | 42 |
| no importance | 19.4% | 29.2% | 49 |
| second part of questionnaire uncompleted i.e. water of no importance | 33.5% } 52.9% | | |

As private abstractors account for 18.2% of all the respondents it was
expected that a close correspondence would occur between private
abstractors, firms that ranked water highly, and firms that felt water
quantity was a crucial location requirement. In fact the picture is rather
more complicated than this. Only 62% of private abstractors gave
water ranks 1, 2 or 3; the remaining 38% indicated that it was not a
vital consideration in the choice of a site. There are two possible
explanations for this variation in ranking. Firstly, there is a distinction
between firms which consciously sought out a site with a suitable water
supply, and those firms which purchased a suitable piece of land and then
availed themselves of the accompanying cheap supply of abstracted water.
The former would rank water highly while the latter may well consider
it to be a minor location factor. Secondly, it is possible that sites,
containing a suitable source of abstraction water, are relatively more
abundant than those satisfying the firms' other location requirements.
Therefore, some private abstractors may give a higher rank to those
factors which are in shorter supply.

Private abstractors account for just over three-quarters of all the
firms ranking water highly, the remainder being made up of firms
supplied solely by local water undertakings. In this remaining quarter
there are three distinct types of firm. Firstly, there are seven very long-
established plants which owe their siting to the availability of water
power. Such firms no longer abstract water for this or any other purpose,
and therefore the high ranking has no present day relevance. Secondly,

there are a number of firms, chiefly in the food, drink and chemical groups, which rely solely on purchased supplies of water but who consider the availability of *potable* water as a major location factor. This type of firm could not entertain a site in a water authority area where a stable and expandable water supply was not guaranteed. A third and increasing group of firms is composed mainly of manufacturers in the plastics and chemical industries, and these have given water a high rank due to their need to dispose of noxious effluent.

There was also no exact correspondence between private abstractors and firms which indicated that water was a crucial location factor, or between those firms giving water a high rank and those stating that it was a crucial factor. It was found, however, that all but one abstractor considered that the availability of water in sufficient quantity and of a suitable quality, or the availability of effluent disposal facilities were crucial or important siting considerations. Likewise all firms giving water ranks 1, 2 or 3 also stated that water quantity, water quality or effluent disposal facilities were crucial or important in their location decisions.

c The results: industry groups[5]
Three factors, land, labour and market were the most crucial ones in the past and present location decisions of firms in every manufacturing group. The chief difference between the industries is in the relative position of these three factors. Land was the most important consideration for firms in the food, chemicals, non-metallic minerals, metals, mechanical engineering and precision engineering groups. In all of these industries over 65% of firms gave land ranks 1 or 2 in both the actual and hypothetical location decisions. Amongst leather and fur producers land appears to have been of first importance in the choice of their present sites, but it would not occupy this position if relocation of the firms took place today. There appears to have been a decline in the relative importance of land as a location factor over time, as in most groups a significantly smaller proportion of firms gave it rank 1 in the hypothetical decision than in the actual past decision. Three industry groups proved exceptions to this case, namely, food, drink and plastics producers.

Labour proved to be the most crucial location factor in both the past and present decisions of clothing manufacturers, 70% of whom gave it ranks 1 or 2 in the past and 90% would give these high rankings if relocation were to occur at the present time. There is evidence that this factor has increased in importance over time, possibly due to the tightening labour market and to the growing managerial awareness of labour shortages. Leather, fur, furniture and metal product firms have indicated that labour would be the most important consideration in any search for a new location. In most other groups (the only exception being printing) it was found that a significantly higher proportion of firms ranked the factor highly in the hypothetical relocation decision than in the actual past decision.

Nearness to market proved to be the most important consideration for printing firms and drink producers in both past and present decisions. There is, however, a very marked increase in the importance of this factor over time, for example, in the past 37% of printers and 44% of drink firms gave market rank 1, but at the present time 75% and 78% respectively would give the factor this ranking. It is suggested that the increased percentage reflects the fact that many firms regard the market as their own established contacts or sales outlets, rather than the number of potential final customers for their output. Therefore, an important element in any relocation choice is the desire to stay in contact with these established outlets. One notably case of this arises in the drink group where manufacturers, especially the brewers, would be most reluctant to move away from their tied public houses, or other established outlets. Once again, in the printing group those papers which serve a limited local area must remain within a relatively confined area to maintain their local character.

The 'accident' factor seems to achieve importance randomly over the industry groups, being ranked of prime importance by between 10% to 30% of firms in each industry group when they considered the past locational decision. Normally the factor was not ranked highly in the present decision as most firms find it inconceivable that relocation could take place on a site selected by 'accident', for personal, or for essentially irrational reasons. A few firms did suggest, however, that they would be reluctant to move away from their founder's home area, or their manager's houses, and have accordingly ranked 'accident' highly in the relocation decision.

None of the remaining factors, raw materials, transport facilities, water supply, and 'other', were given high rankings by the majority of firms in any industry group. 'Other' factors rarely were important locational considerations, although government direction, or the danger of bomb damage did influence the decisions of one or two firms in most groups. Government direction has been particularly important in the relatively modern rubber and plastics group, as it was the most important influence on the actual decision of 16.7% of the firms.

There was a wide variation within each industry group in the ranks given to raw materials, transport facilities and water supply, and there was also a wide variation between groups in the relative importance of these three factors. Raw materials appears to be the most important of the three in the past location of paper, plastics and non-metallic minerals firms, but in both the paper and plastics groups water supply becomes a more vital factor when relocation is considered. Water supply is also most important in the past location of food and drink producers and in the possible future location of textile manufacturers. In every industry group, except chemicals, fewer firms considered that transport facilities were

**Figure 10a A histogram showing the variation in the ranks given to water in paper firms.**

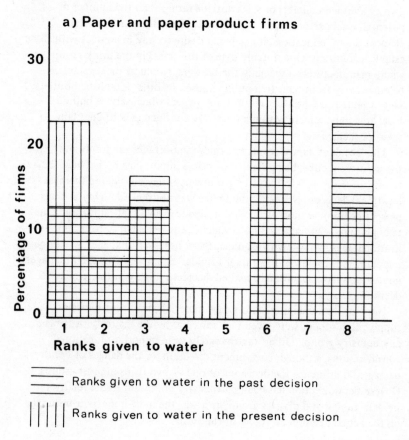

**Figure 10b A histogram showing the variation in the ranks given to water by printing firms**

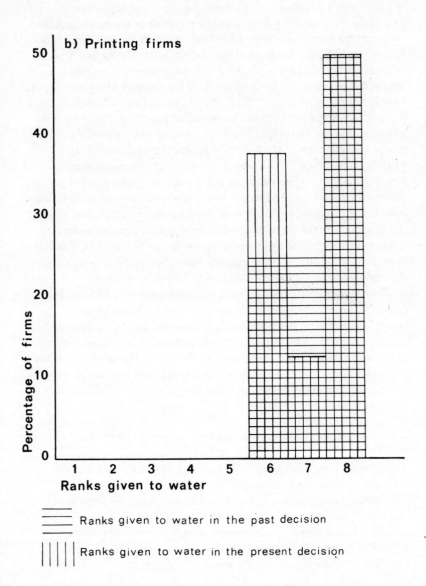

b) Printing firms

Percentage of firms

Ranks given to water

═══ Ranks given to water in the past decision

||||| Ranks given to water in the present decision

the prime location factor than gave raw materials or water supply 1st rank. But it was usual for transport to be given ranks 2, 3 and 4: in other words although the factor was rarely the most vital consideration it was usually a moderately important factor in all industry groups. It would be difficult to assert that water supplies are generally more or less important to firms than the availability or cost of raw materials or transport facilities. Although the mean rank for water is lower than that for the other two factors, the standard deviation of the ranks is greater in the majority of groups. In general it would appear that water supplies are a more specialized requirement; the availability of the resource being fundamental to only a small proportion of firms within each industry. Therefore, there is a tendency for water either to be ranked of great importance or of no importance at all. The range of rankings given to water within the industry groups is a reflection of the variety of products manufactured. This variation is particularly noticeable in the paper group, where there is a clear differentiation between raw paper producers, who give the resource high ranks, and paper product manufacturers, who consider the availability of water as a minor location factor; figure 10(a) clearly shows this distribution. On the other hand in some industry groups water is uniformly unimportant and there is little variation in the ranks. The best example of this is the printing industry (see figure 10(b), although both the engineering groups have a similar distribution of rankings.

Throughout the industry group tabulations there is no clear evidence that water supply has become a more important location factor in recent years. Only in the paper group is there any significant increase in the proportion of firms ranking water as the most important factor, but even in this group there is no overall increase in the number of firms giving water ranks 1, 2 or 3. Any shortage of suitable abstraction sites has not resulted in a conscious re-evaluation of water as a location factor.

d The results: size groups
All the respondent firms were placed into size groups on the basis of the number of persons employed. Although it is recognized that employment is only one element in firm size, it was the best available surrogate in the absence of output or capital stock data. Frequency distributions of the ranks given to each location factor by firms in each size group were then calculated.

It was found that as in the industry groups the most important factors in each of the size categories were land, labour, market and 'accident'. Land was consistently the most highly ranked factor, being of prime importance to over 30% of firms in every size group. There was no consistent variation over the size categories in the proportion of firms ranking land highly. In fact this lack of a trend over size also occurred for the labour and market factors. This suggests that the importance of these three location factors is determined by some characteristic of the firms other than the number of persons employed. The accidental element in factory location was important in the past decision of between 10% and 30% of firms in each size category, with a tendency for the factor to be more inportant in very small firms, employing under 50 persons.

In the case of water supply there is a very noticeable tendency for the importance of water to vary with size. This can be seen from table 22, which shows how the mean rank for water decreases as the labour force increases. The means are inflated by the number of firms which rely solely on bought supplies and do not consider water availability at all when seeking a new location; in other words the standard deviation of the rankings is large.

Table 22. The mean rank given to water supply in each of the size groups

| number of employees | mean rank in past decision | mean rank in present decision | number of firms in each size group |
|---|---|---|---|
| 15– 49 | 6.6 | 6.5 | 37 |
| 50– 99 | 6.4 | 6.1 | 54 |
| 100–199 | 6.1 | 5.7 | 48 |
| 200–299 | 6.0 | 5.4 | 26 |
| 300–499 | 5.7 | 5.2 | 36 |
| 500–999 | 5.9 | 5.4 | 28 |
| over 1000 | 3.9 | 4.0 | 24 |

(i.e. the lower the mean the greater the importance of water.)

It would appear that the availability of water supply and/or effluent disposal facilities is one of the most important factors considered in the locational decisions of firms employing over 1,000 persons. When these large firms located to their present sites water supply was the second most important consideration after the availability of the land, and 60% of firms ranked water 1, 2 or 3. The resource seems to have declined in relative importance over time, as in the relocation decision the reluctance of firms to move away from established contacts increased the position of the market factor at the expense of water; only 50% of firms ranked

**Figure 11 Cumulative frequency curves showing the ranks given to water by firms in the size groups.**

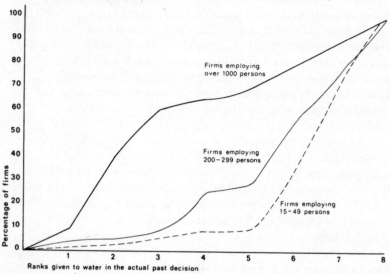

water highly in the hypothetical relocation decision. Figure 11 clearly illustrates the much greater importance of water supply to large firms than to small ones. The figure shows the cumulative percentage of firms giving each ranking to water and the concave shape of the curve for firms with over 1,000 employees implies that water is ranked of great importance by the majority of concerns.

e The results: age groups

In this section of the locational analysis the respondent firms were re-categorized on the basis of the length of time they have occupied their present sites. Frequency distributions of the ranks given to each factor by the firms in the different groups were calculated once again. One prominent feature of these distributions is that there is a much greater variation in the importance of factors between age groups than there was between size groups.

The availability of land and premises appears to have increased in importance over time, the greatest increase having taken place from the beginning of the present century until 1960. Only 27% of firms established between 1850 and 1917, and no firms located before this period, ranked land as the most important factor in the choice of their

present site. On the other hand over 50% of firms established between
1945 and 1959 considered that land was the most vital factor. This
increase in importance over time is probably due to a combination of
trends. Firstly, competition for land has become increasingly intense as
industrialization and urbanization have proceeded. Secondly, there has
been a growing emphasis on land-use planning, which has increased
control over industrial building, making the amount of land available
for development more limited. A third possibility is that the nature of
industry has changed over the years and with it there has been an
alteration in firms' space requirements; the development of large scale
integrated works may well have had this effect. Finally, it may be the
case that the increase in the importance of land is more apparent than
real being the results of imperfect knowledge about the true location
factors. The more remote the past locational decision the less likely
the rankings are to be accurate; managements' rationalization of past
motives may have increased the importance of other factors, including
'accident', at the expense of land. While this source of bias must remain
a possibility, it is thought that an actual increase in the position of land
as a location factor has probably occurred over time. Whether this trend
will continue into the future is open to question as in the age group 1960
to 1966 a significantly lower proportion (30.8%) of firms ranked land of
premier importance. This may be due to an increase in the relative
positions of labour and government direction.

Labour appears to have markedly increased in importance over time
as a location factor. Not only does the factor have a higher proportion
of high rankings in the hypothetical relocation decision than in the actual
past location, but also there is an increasing proportion of firms ranking
the factor highly as the age of the firm decreases. Most of the increase
in the importance of labour has occurred after the second world war.
Before 1939 between 6% and 8% of firms considered that the
availability and cost of labour was the most vital location factor, but
13% of firms established between 1945 and 1949 ranked labour of
first importance, as did 23% of post 1960 firms.

The position of the market factor in the locational decisions of
managers appears to have remained much more stable over time than
either land or labour. There was, however, a temporary but very marked
decline in the importance of the market for firms establishing new
factories during the second world war. Defence considerations and
government direction were of prime importance during this period. In
all other age categories between 14% and 24% of firms ranked market

as first factor, whereas during the war years no firm placed it in this position.

The three previously discussed factors, land, labour and market, have had the greatest influence on the location of firms within each of the age categories, with the notable exception of firms established before 1850 (see below). In all the age groups very few firms consider that the availability or cost of raw materials has played a vital part in the choice of a factory site. Before 1939 less than 10% of firms gave the factor first rank and this percentage has fallen to below 5% since that date. Transport facilities and costs have also been placed in rank 1 by less than 5% of the concerns in each age group. It would appear that the accident factor has contributed to the actual location decision in all of the age categories, but that it was most important in the siting of the older firms. This feature could possibly imply that modern firms are less likely to be swayed by 'accidental' factors; that managers now undertake a more rational appraisal of their requirements when making any decision to locate. On the other hand it could be the case that the older the firm, the less likely the managers are to know the true reasons for the location and the more prone they are to attribute it to accident. Alternatively, in the newer firms, the person responsible for the choice of the site may well also answer the questionnaire and he may be unwilling to acknowledge that 'accidental' elements contributed to the locational decision. The influence of 'other' factors was most marked during the war years, when government direction and the fear of bomb damage were two important considerations. This category also appears to be increasing its position in the more recent decisions; industrial development certificates, development grants and the need to obtain planning permission all have an increasing role to play in industrial location decisions.

Most firms which have been established during the twentieth century consider that the availability of water supplies and effluent disposal facilities was a minor element in the search for and choice of their sites. Not more than 1 or 2 firms in each age category after 1918 have ranked the resource of premier importance. As figure 12 illustrates water supply made its largest contribution to the locational decisions of firms established on their present sites before the first world war. The resource was given ranks 1, 2 or 3 by 19% of firms established between 1850 and 1918, and by 60% of firms built before 1850. In the latter age group water was the most important factor in the locational decision. As table 23 shows, in the actual past decision the mean rank given to water by

**Figure 12 Cumulative frequency curves showing the ranks given to water by firms in the age groups**

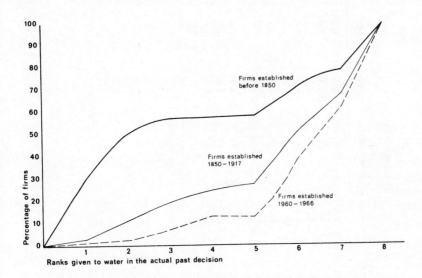

firms built before 1850 is lower than that for any other factor. Water would not, however, be such a vital factor if relocation of the factory occurred today.

Water's importance in the location of these old established firms is probably accounted for by the general paucity of public water supply facilities at this time. Although some private water companies were operating in a few urban areas before the nineteenth century, it was not until the mid century that water companies and public water authorities became a general feature (110 p 14). The development of a public system of water supply increased the ubiquity of the resource for most firms, although manufacturers had no rights to supply until 1945 (116 p 29).

Firms requiring small gallonages of water were usually able to obtain their needs from the public water supply industry, and water became of minor locational importance. Water is not, however, a single uniform and interchangeable product, and so firms requiring water in quantities or in quality exceeding that economically purchased from public suppliers, do not find the resource ubiquitous. Water is, therefore, still a relatively important location factor for these firms as the chosen new site must

Table 23. Mean factor ranks by age groups

| date of establishment on present site | location decision | mean ranks for | | | | | | | |
|---|---|---|---|---|---|---|---|---|---|
| | | water | land | labour | market | raw materials | transport | 'other' | accident |
| 1960–1966 | past | 6.6 | 3.0 | 3.3 | 3.4 | 5.0 | 4.5 | 6.3 | 6.1 |
| | present | 6.6 | 2.6 | 2.9 | 3.2 | 4.8 | 4.1 | 6.6 | 6.5 |
| 1944–1959 | past | 6.2 | 2.3 | 3.2 | 4.0 | 4.7 | 4.7 | 7.1 | 6.2 |
| | present | 6.0 | 2.0 | 2.5 | 4.0 | 4.6 | 4.5 | 7.0 | 7.4 |
| 1939–1943 | past | 5.9 | 2.2 | 3.5 | 4.4 | 5.2 | 5.0 | 5.1 | 6.5 |
| | present | 4.8 | 2.2 | 2.4 | 4.5 | 4.5 | 4.1 | 6.9 | 7.8 |
| 1918–1938 | past | 5.8 | 2.4 | 3.3 | 3.0 | 4.3 | 4.5 | 7.0 | 6.4 |
| | present | 5.3 | 2.3 | 2.4 | 3.1 | 4.2 | 4.3 | 7.2 | 7.4 |
| 1850–1917 | past | 6.0 | 3.3 | 4.1 | 3.4 | 4.9 | 4.9 | 7.4 | 5.4 |
| | present | 5.4 | 3.1 | 2.6 | 2.5 | 4.8 | 3.8 | 6.8 | 7.7 |
| pre–1850 | past | 3.7 | 4.3 | 4.5 | 4.8 | 4.9 | 4.8 | 6.9 | 5.9 |
| | present | 3.9 | 2.4 | 3.3 | 3.2 | 4.5 | 4.4 | 7.2 | 7.6 |

have access to a suitable source of abstraction water. The resource does, therefore, have some part to play in a location theory which is designed to describe and explain the decisions of manager. But with the development of public water supply facilities the demand for water is relatively easy to satisfy compared with the demands for land or a labour supply.

It was concluded from the frequency tabulations by industry group that there was no evidence to suggest that water is becoming more important as a location factor. The results of the age group computations support this conclusion; in fact they lead to the suggestion that water is a less important factor at the present time than it was before 1850. This is not to say that water has declined absolutely in importance but that it has decreased relative to the other location factors. Although it cannot be concluded that in future firms will not re-evaluate the position of water as a location factor, it would require a strong reversal of the present trend for this to occur. Certainly no re-evaluation is likely if water supplies are expanded to meet all foreseeable needs.

**Determinants of intra-industry variations in the ranking of water**
Least squares regression, using both simple and multiple equation forms, was employed to determine which internal characteristics of firms affect their rankings of location factors; the same method was used previously in the estimation of the determinants of the quantity of water demanded by firms. Three of the variables used in the quantity regressions were also introduced into the location explanatory equations, namely the number of persons employed, the tonnage of raw materials entering the manufacturing process, and the length of occupance of the present site. These variables were used because employment and tonnage had proved to be closely related to the quantity of water demanded and because a firm's age had emerged in the description of ranks as having an influence on the locational importance of water. In addition the proportional contribution to total costs of raw material, labour, power, and transport costs were included as independent explanatory variables. *Prima facie* it was thought that firms using large quantities of power and raw materials would rank water of more importance than firms in which labour costs were the greatest contributors to total costs; these expectations were not in fact borne out by the results.

1 *Statistical problems*
As has been mentioned previously the use of least squares regression

means that care must be taken in the setting up of the equation forms
to ensure that the assumptions underlying this technique are fulfilled
as far as possible.[6] Any deviation from the assumptions may affect
the significance of the observed relationships, and the results must be
assessed accordingly.

A number of statistical problems which arose in the analysis of the
determinants of the quantity of water taken by firms also occurred in
the location regressions. The first problem was that a dummy or proxy
variable for industry group was not available and this has meant that
it was not possible to find any meaningful relationships between the
explanatory variables and the ranks given to water by *all* firms. None of
the regressions produced a significant result at the 0.95 level of
probability when information from every respondent firm was used.
Manufacturers had, therefore to be split up into industry groups, and the
scope of the analysis had to be narrowed to the determination of the
factors causing intra-industry variations in the ranking of water as a
location factor.

The second problem of multicollinearity (intercorrelation between
the independent variables) was also present in the ranking analysis. In
fact it is a more serious problem here than it was in the estimation of
the determinants of the quantity of water used. Not only does
intercorrelation exist between the tonnage of raw materials taken and
and the number of persons employed in a few of the industry groups, but
also there is inevitably a strong relationship between the various elements
which contribute to the total cost of production. As transport costs, raw
material costs and so on are expressed as percentages of one total, an
increase in one percentage must result in a decrease in all others, and
therefore multicollinearity must occur. Wherever possible the use of more
than one of the cost proportions in the same equation was avoided; this
has probably meant a lowering of the explanatory value of the multiple
regression models, but it has made the results less subject to error.

Autocorrelation is another possible source of error, and so each
best-fit equation was tested by using the Durbin-Watson statistic
(29 part II, p 173). In most industry groups autocorrelation was not
found to be present in the regressions and, therefore, it can be concluded
that no important independent variable that could *systematically* affect
the residuals has been omitted from the analysis. This is not to suggest
that no other factors have influenced the ranks given to water, but that
any other influences do not act in a systematic manner.

The final statistical problem encountered in the analysis of water as a locational factor stems from the use of ordinal data (i.e. information based on rankings rather than numerical values). The use of an ordinal scale has four main disadvantages:—

1 It shows relative and not absolute importance. For example, a rank of 1 may imply that a particular factor was the least unimportant of a set of unimportant factors, or the most crucial of a crucial set of factors. It does not, therefore, permit comparison of degrees of importance, in an absolute sense, between different firms, or even for one firm at different times.

2 It does not quantify the degree of difference between the factors. For example, for one firm the difference in the importance of the 1st and 2nd factors may be marginal, whereas for another firm it may be exceptionally wide.

3 The ranks can only be integer values, and this presents a problem in a statistical analysis since the discrete nature of the values may lead to distortions of the regression line.

4 Finally, as the ordinals are related to each other, any discovered relationship between one of the independent variables and the ranks for one of the location factors may in fact reflect a strong relationship between that independent variable and one of the other ranked factors. For example, the proportion of raw material cost in the total cost may be related positively to the rank of water (i.e. the greater the proportion of raw material costs the lower the importance of water), but this relationship may only be derived from the relationship between the same independent variable and the rank of raw materials. The greater proportion raw material costs are to total cost, the higher the raw material factor is ranked, and this in turn may mean a decline in the ranking of water supply.

Despite these problems, which must be taken into account when the results are assessed, it is hoped that the ranking approach to a firms' locational decision will produce some meaningful results. It is certainly one of the few accessible methods of quantifying what is essentially qualitative data.

*2 The factors determining the rank given to water supply*[7]
The length of time that a firm has occupied its present site proved to be the best explanatory variable of the ranks given to water by firms in the largest number of industry groups (see Table 24). Age produced the highest levels of explanation and the greatest degrees of significance in the plastics, mechanical engineering, clothing, leather and fur industries.[8]

**Table 24.** The most significant variables explaining the rankings given to water by firms in each industry group

| industry group | most significant variable | other significant variables | best-fit simple equation form | $R^2$ value for simple regression | | $R^2$ value for multiple regression | |
|---|---|---|---|---|---|---|---|
| | | | | past % | present % | past % | present % |
| food | — | — | — | — | — | — | —* |
| drink | percentage of transport costs | percentage of power costs, employment, tonnage | $R_w = a + b\%t$ | 50.2 | 38.0 | 92.4 | 86.1 |
| leather, fur, and clothing | age | none | $R_w = a + bA^2$ | 53.2 | 40.0 | 75.6 | 62.4 |
| furniture and timber | percentage of power costs | age | $R_w = a + b\%P$ | 30.5 | 31.2 | 90.5 | 78.3 |
| plastics and rubber | age | none | $R_w = a + bA^3$ | 42.1 | 58.6 | 48.9 | 63.2 |
| paper and paper products | — | — | — | — | — | — | —* |
| chemicals | employment | percentage of raw material costs | $R_w = a + b\log E$ | 6.3 | 11.1 | 12.1 | 15.0 |
| non-metallic minerals | ton-input | age | $R_w = a + b\log T$ | 0 | 41.8 | 0 | 52.5 |
| metals and metal products | employment | none | $R_w = a + bE$ | 19.1 | 16.2 | 43.7 | 34.6 |
| mechanical engineering | age | percentage of raw material costs | $R_w = a + bA^3$ | 41.7 | 41.4 | 62.1 | 62.2 |
| precision engineering | ton-input | percentage of labour costs | $R_w = a + bT$ | 0 | 34.4† | 0 | 61.4† |

*For these two groups no significant relationships were established.
†These results are badly distorted by autocorrelation.

In all these groups the regression coefficient $b$ was negative, which indicates that the longer a firm has been established on its present site the more important water is likely to be as a location factor. This result is in accord with the findings of the frequency distributions previously discussed. (p120-1.)

In the combined *clothing* and *leather* group age of the firm was most significantly related to the rank given to water in both past and present location decisions when a form of quadratic equation was used.[9] An equation $R_w = a + bA^2$ explained 53.2% of the variation in the position' of water in the actual location decision and 40% of the variation in the hypothetical relocation decision. The shape of the curve described by this equation form implies that the rank given to water falls as age increases, but that the rate of fall slackens off at the oldest age levels (i.e. pre −1850). In other words the oldest established firms found that water was a much more vital factor in their choice of a site, than more recently developed firms. It was found that the level of explanation of the variation in ranks could be increased by adding other independent variables to the regression model. Two additional variables were added, namely the tonnage of raw materials used and the percentage of labour costs in the total costs. Neither of these variables were significant but the equation $R_w = a + bA^2 + cT^2 + d\%L^2$ did explain 75.6% of the variation in ranks in the past decision and 62.4% of that in the relocation decision.[10]

The age of *plastics* firms was best related to the rankings given to water supply in the past and at the present time, when the equation form $R_w = a + bA^3$ was used. This equation probably results from the highly diverse nature of the firms within this group, which includes raw plastics producers, plastic products firms and rubber manufacturers. The simple regression using age as the sole independent variable explained 42.1% of the variation in the past decision rank and 58.6% of the present ranking. Many multiple regression equations, using employment, tonnage and the proportions of total cost as additional variables, were run but little improvement of the level of explanation resulted. The most successful multiple regression model $R_w = a + bA^3 + cE^3 + dT^3$ only increased the $R^2$ value to 48.9% for the past ranking and 63.2% for the present ranking, an increase in both cases of under 8% over the simple equation form.

A similar equation form also best described the relationship between the age of firms in the *mechanical engineering* group and the past and present ranks given to water. 41.7% of the variation in the past rankings and 41.4% of the variation in the present day ranks was explained by the simple regression equation $R_w = a + bA^3$. These levels of explanation are markedly improved when other variables were added to the basic equation. The highest $R^2$ values, which were not affected by multicollinearity, were obtained using the equation $R_w = a + bA^3 + cE^3 + d\%M^3 + eT^3$. This model explained 62.1% of the variation in the ranks given to water in the past and 62.2% of the variation in the present rankings.

Age of the firms was also a significant determinant of the ranks given to water by *non-metallic mineral concerns*; in this case, however, the level of explanation was lower than that achieved when tonnage of raw materials was used as the sole independent variable. In this industry the regression coefficient of the relationship between age and rank was negative, thus producing an expected shape of curve, with the importance of water increasing as the age of the firm increases. The best-fit equation was $R_w = a + b \log A$, but levels of explanation were poor, being below 20% for both the past and present day rankings.

In the *timber and furniture* group the length of time the firm had been established on its present site was also significantly related to the rankings, but the $b$ coefficient was positive. This means that the more modern the firm the more highly water will be regarded as a location factor. Two possible explanations of this positive relationship were suggested by the Technical Director of one large furniture firm, which was selected for a test interview. Firstly, furniture makers have become increasingly aware of fire risk problems and at the same time local authorities have introduced more stringent fire regulations. The provision of a high pressure, reliable supply of water may now be an important location factor, especially if new high pressure pipes have to be laid onto the site. One of the sampled furniture firms claims to have rejected a possible site for a branch plant because the local water undertaking refused to lay the new pipe unless the firm paid the costs in full. The site finally chosen was in a rural area and, as the local authority wished to encourage industrial development, it was prepared to pay for the provision of a high pressure pipeline and a water tower to regulate pressure in the pipe and fire sprinklers.[11] A second possible factor contributing to the increased importance of water to recently established firms is that most firms now use relatively large gallonages in spray booths, whereas in the past dry booths were used.[12] The relationships between the age of a furniture firm and the ranks given to water in the past and present are best described by simple linear equations

($R_w = a + bA$) but the level of explanation was poor in both cases, being 21% and 23.2% respectively.

The number of persons employed proved to be the best explanatory variable of the ranks allotted to water supply by firms in the *metals and chemicals* groups. In both these groups, the levels of explanation were poor, although the observed relationships were significant at the 0.95% level of probability. It was found that the best-fit equation form in the metals industry was linear, and the simple regression explained 19.1% of the variation in the past rankings, and 16.2% in the present ranks. In both cases the established relationship was negative, which means that as metal producing plants increase in size water becomes a more important factor in their locational decisions. The regressions for the *chemical* industry also produced a negative relationship between employment and the rank for water, but in this group the best-fit equation was $R_w = a + b \log E$. Levels of explanation achieved by this equation were low, 6.3% of the variation in the past rankings was explained and 11.1% of that in the present ranking. Multiple regression models were only able to increase the level of explanation slightly.

A third independent variable to be related to the rank given to water was the tonnage of raw materials used in the manufacturing process. This factor was negatively related to the rank which *precision engineering* and *non-metallic mineral* firms would give to water if they were to search for a new site at the present time. In the *non-metallic minerals* group a logarithmically transformed equation $R_w = a + b \log T$, produced the highest level of explanation (41.8%) and this was increased to 52.5% when other independent variables were added to produce a multiple regression model ($R_w = a + b \log T + c \log A + d \log E + e \log \%M$). It was found that the results for the precision engineering group were badly distorted by autocorrelation[13] and therefore, there is no assurance that the observed relationship between tonnage of raw materials and water's rank is a significant one, as autocorrelation affects the estimate of the standard error.

The percentage of transport costs in total production costs was significantly related to the ranks given to water in both the past and present locational decisions of firms in the *drink industry*. A simple linear equation produced an $R^2$ value of 0.502 in the past rank regression, and one of 0.38 in the present rank computations. In both cases the established relationship was negative, which implies that water becomes a more important location factor as the proportion of transport costs increases. One possible explanation of this is that the firms with the highest transport costs are those that incorporate large quantities of water in their final product. If this were the case transport costs would be dependent on water usage, rather than being an independent, explanatory variable of water's importance.

In the *furniture industry* the percentage of power costs in the total costs was a significant independent variable. A simple linear equation gave an $R^2$ value of 0.305 (30%) in the regression on the past ranks and 0.315 in the present rank regression. Levels of explanation were greatly improved when further variables were added to the simple linear equation. The model $R_w = a + b \% P + c \% M + dA + eT^{14}$ explained 90.5% of the variation in the ranks given to water in the past, and 78.3% for the present ranks.

It was not possible to establish any meaningful significant relationships between any of the independent variables and the ranks given to water in the *paper* and *food* industry groups. This suggests that the rankings given to water must be determined by factors not included in the regression equations, but as no autocorrelation was present in the regressions it is unlikely that any excluded factor has influenced the rankings in a systematic way.

Although it was possible to establish significant relationships between some of the independent explanatory variables and the ranks given to water, the levels of explanation were generally too low to use the equations for predictive purposes. The length of time that a firm has been located on its present site proved to be the best explanatory variable in the plastics, mechanical engineering, clothing, leather and fur groups; it was also significant in the non-metallic minerals, and furniture industries. Most of the other variables only achieved significance in one or at the most two industry groups. Employment, for example, was related to the ranks of water in the metals and chemical groups, while ton input was linked with the rankings given by precision engineering and non-metallic mineral firms. The proportions of transport and power costs achieved significance in the drink and furniture industries respectively.

## Conclusion

In this chapter an attempt has been made to analyse the role of water supply and effluent disposal facilities in the location of industry. A distinction has been made between spatial and behavioural theories of location, and the importance of water varies with the type of theory which is being developed. It is thought that water probably has little relevance as a location factor in spatial theories, or at least in theories which have been developed to consider regional development in Britain at the present time. However, in the future, the role of water in spatial patterns of industrial development may have to be re-evaluated as suitable abstraction sites become scarce.

On the other hand if a location theory is behavioural, that is, it is designed to explain why individual firms reach their locational decisions, the water supply factor may well be a more important consideration. In the simple micro-locational model outlined previously it was claimed that siting factors are the most important elements in firms' location decisions. Most business managers only begin to search for a new location when all possibilities of expansion on the present site have been exhausted, and they will usually seek an undeveloped site or an existing building as near to the present factory as possible, the maintenance of contacts with the parent plant or with existing market outlets is considered of prime importance. The general area of location being given, the main locational problem facing the firms is to find a suitable site. The replies from the 'Industrial Survey' were used to find which are the most important requirements of the firms in their choice of sites.

Land emerged as the most crucial consideration for the majority of firms. Many firms claimed that it proved difficult to find a piece of land of sufficient size, for which planning permission was available. Other important factors for most firms were the maintenance of existing market contacts, and the availability of a suitable labour force. Some firms wished to re-locate very close to their original factory in order to retain their present workers. The 'accident' factor was also an important one, especially in the actual past locational decision. These four factors proved to be the chief considerations of firms in most industry, size and age groups.

Water was clearly not a critical factor in the locational decision of most firms, although it was ranked on a par with raw materials and transport, two factors which have traditionally been regarded as vital by theorists. One important feature of the results is that large firms employing over 1000 persons do find water an important consideration. It would appear that water supply and effluent disposal facilities have declined in importance as locational factors relative to the other factors over the past 100 years. Water was most vital in the past locational decisions of firms established before 1850. Since that time the extension of public water supply facilities has increased the ubiquity of water, and

F

therefore has increased the ease with which industrial water requirements are satisfied. In the future, however, firms are requiring private abstraction water may find sources increasingly difficult to find and this may cause the factor to become a more important locational consideration, at least for large firms using water for cooling or in the manufacturing process.

Finally in this chapter, an attempt was made to determine the reasons why there were wide intra-industry variations in the ranks given to water. *Prima facie* it was thought that the number of persons employed, and the tonnage of raw materials used would explain much of the variation, while the age of the firm would also be a significant factor. In fact it was found that the age of the firm was the most successful determinant of the rankings in the greatest number of industry groups. Employment, tonnage and the proportions of power and transport costs in total production costs, were also significant independent variables in some industries. Levels of explanation were generally low and no attempt will be made to use the equations for predictive purposes.

# Chapter 6

# Forecasts and predictions

In the previous chapters the economic characteristics of the water industry as a whole have been considered, the demand for water by manufacturing industry has been described and analysed, and the influence of water as a location factor has been examined. Hitherto the discussion has been essentially static, relating to the years 1965-66, during which the water statistics were collected and the 'Industrial Survey' was taken. The present chapter projects the analysis into the future by using the results of the preceding analysis, as well as the replies to some of the questions in the 'Industrial Survey',(see Appendix B, questions B,2, 3, 4 & 7). An attempt will be made to forecast the quantity of water demanded by various types of manufacturing unit. The possible effects of water planning and controls on the demand for industrial supplies will be discussed. Finally the possible trends in the influence of water on industrial location will be considered.

**Demand forecasts**

*1 Analytical limitations*
An important limitation on the use of the results from the quantity regression analysis to forecast future industrial demands for water arises from the fact that cross-sectional rather than time-series data were used. In other words the study shows how the variables were related across firms at one period of time, but this is not necessarily the same thing as the relationship between the same variables over time. Therefore, when attempting to forecast from the results of a cross-sectional analysis, the assumption must be made that the same functional relationships between the variables exist over time. For example, when the results of a regression of the quantity of water purchased on employment are used to forecast the future demands for water from firms of given sizes, the assumption must be made that no factors have altered the slope of the established relationship, or have shifted the regression line. This case is illustrated in figure 13.

At the present time firm X takes $o - c$ million gallons of water per annum and employs $o - a$ persons, while firm Y takes $o - d$ million gallons and

**Figure 13 A change in the relationship between employment and the quantity of water purchased.**

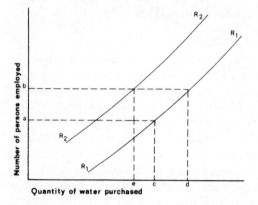

employs $o - b$ persons. From this a forecast could be made that when at some future time firm X expands to employ $o - b$ persons it will also purchase $o - d$ million gallons of water per annum. The accuracy of this estimate will depend on whether changes in technology or in the economic and social conditions have affected the relationship between the two variables. During the period of time that firm X was expanding to employ $o - b$ persons the fundamental determinants of the regression parameters may have been altered. For example a change in water technology could cause the best-fit regression line to shift from $R_1$ to $R_2$ (i.e. a saving in the water used by each employee would occur). This being the case firm X would only take $o - e$ million gallons of water per annum when it employes $o - b$ persons.

The *ceteris paribus* assumption therefore limits the general applicability of the analysis results to situations in which the underlying relationships have not been significantly altered over time. It is thought that acceptably accurate forecasts would be obtained at the present time if the results were used to estimate the water requirements of newly established firms, firms expanding their output and firms intending to relocate. Only three years have elapsed since the 'Industrial Survey' was taken and so it is doubtful whether the regression parameters will have yet been altered significantly, but the further forward in time the forecast is made the more liable it will be to error. On the other hand it seems reasonable to suggest that the results will not lose all value for forecasting in the future as they can be used to produce a base figure, which can then be adjusted to account for the effects of any technological, political, economic or social changes, which may have occurred since 1965-6, when the survey was taken. In addition the results provide an indication of the direction and magnitude of any shifts in the demand curve for water, which are caused by changes in the underlying conditions.

A second limitation in using the results of the demand analysis to forecast industrial water consumption is that some of the best-fit regression equations produced low levels of explanation ($R^2$). Although the established relationships were significant the observations were highly scattered about the regression line. The independent variables used were not able to explain enough of the variation in the quantity of water taken to make the regression equation a valuable forecasting model. Forecasting errors probably would be too large and would occur too frequently if equation forms with $R^2$ values of less than 0.60 (60%) were used. In addition it is likely that the forecast results can only be treated with a high degree of confidence when the equation used has an $R^2$ value of over 0.75 (75%).

It was found that no demand forecasts could be made for industry as a whole if the 0.60 level of explanation was taken as a cut-off value, below which the regression equation was discarded as a forecasting tool. As table 19, page 100 shows, the best-fit explanatory equations only explain 34.9% of the variation in the quantity of water *purchased* by all firms and only 16.6% of the variation in the level of *private abstraction.* In the same way no demand forecasts can be made for firms in the plastics and engineering sub-groups, in which the levels of explanation are below 45%.

## 2 *The forecasts*

Water engineers frequently complain that manufacturers are unwilling or unable to estimate a proposed factory's full capacity water requirements. When a firm applies for planning permission to establish a branch plant (relocate a parent factory or to extend an existing plant's capacity) it often requests a water supply that is only adequate for the first few years of production, during which the factory is operating below capacity. Further and possibly large supplies of water are then demanded when the firm is fully established and is approaching full capacity output. The local undertaking concerned may be placed in a difficult supply position, at least in the short-run, if the firm's demands are met, and if they are refused the factory would be working inefficiently. It is therefore important to be able to estimate the full capacity water requirements of proposed manufacturing plants as it will enable the local undertaking to plan the development of its supply capacity accordingly. The construction of additional storage or pumping capacity would only be justified, however, if the firm is prepared to pay for any additional costs of supply imposed by its demands (i.e. if the firm is prepared to pay the marginal cost of its water supply). This point has been discussed in detail in Chapter 2, pages 15-16.

In the subsequent sections of this chapter it is proposed to give tentative estimates of the minimum water requirements of firms in various industry groups. In addition models which could enable planners and water undertakings to estimate the likely water requirements of newly established or expanding firms will be discussed.

a The chemical industry (pp 68-74[1]).

As table 19 shows, the tonnage of raw materials entering the manufacturing process is closely associated with the quantity of water *purchased* by chemical firms from local water undertakings. The best-fit equation form, $Q^2 = a + bT$, explains 97.3% of the variation in the level of water purchased and therefore it can be used as a forecasting model with a high degree of confidence. Although a firm may be unable to estimate a plant's future water requirements, it is argued here that the manufacturers should be able to estimate the tonnage of raw materials that will be handled by a newly established plant during the initial period of development, and also the tonnage that the plant will be capable of handling when full output capacity is reached. The water undertakings can then use these tonnage estimates to derive approximate figures for both the initial and full capacity water demands of chemical plants.

It is unlikely that any chemical firm employing over 15 persons will demand very much less than 557,000 gallons of water per annum from the local water undertaking, irrespective of the quantity of raw materials entering the manufacturing process. Before a chemical firm can operate efficiently this threshold quantity of water must be purchased each year.[2] Most firms will, in fact, demand larger gallonages than this, and the demand can be approximated by adding the estimated tonnage of raw materials used to the equation $Q^2 = 310662811 + 15121172 \, (T)$, where both $Q^2$ and $T$ are in units of 1000. Supposing a firm used 6,000 tons of raw materials, which is above the average (4,000 tons) for chemical manufacturers, then it would probably demand approximately 20 million gallons of water per annum from the local undertaking.[3] As ton-input is positively related to the quantity of water purchased any firm using less than 6,000 tons will take under 20 mgy, and any firm handling over 6,000 tons will demand over 20 mgy. The rate of increase in the quantity of water demanded does, however, slow down as higher levels of ton-input are reached.

It is also possible to give some tentative estimate of the quantity of water which a chemical firm would *wish* to *abstract* from privately owned sources of supply. First it can be said that a chemical firm is unlikely to wish to abstract water privately unless over approximately 2,700 tons of raw materials are used each year. This, in fact, excludes a large proportion of chemical firms, as the majority handle only small quantities of light raw materials. Such firms normally require relatively small quantities of water and find it is more convenient (and/or economic) to purchase all their requirements. Chemical firms using over 2,700 tons of raw materials will probably wish to abstract approximately 28 million gallons of water per annum for each additional 1000 tons used.[4] A firm handling 6,000 tons of raw materials will, therefore, wish to abstract approximately 110 million gallons of water per annum.

Forecasts of the quantity of water *abstracted* privately, however, will be more liable to error than those of the quantity of water purchased. In the case of chemical firms this is in part due to the fact that only 7 sample firms owned private sources of supply; the regression line was, therefore, only fitted to 8 points (the 7 firms plus a cluster of non-abstractors, see figure 6 page 72). The second reason for the greater liability to error is applicable to all industry groups, not just to chemical firms. It is only possible to indicate the quantity of water that a firm would *wish* to abstract privately if an abstraction licence was made available, no guide to the actual amount that will be taken can be given. Since the 1963 *Water Resources Act* the individual firm is no longer the sole determinator of the quantity of water abstracted from private sources of supply; a final decision is made by the relevant river authority. This means that factors influencing the demand for abstracted water supplies have changed since the survey period, 1965-6, and therefore the *ceteris paribus* assumption no longer holds. When the 'Industrial Survey' was taken the firms had not yet been affected by the provisions of the 1963 Act, since the majority of abstractors were entitled to receive licences of right. Only firms seeking to expand their water withdrawals or to relocate their premises will feel the full impact of the new Act. The extent of the divergence between a firm's desired level of abstraction and the actual quantity taken will depend on the procedure introduced by the river authorities to allocate scarce resources between competitors.

Under the 1963 *Water Resources Act* abstractors will be required to pay for withdrawals on a quantity taken basis. When this charging scheme comes into operation the deviation between the quantity demanded and the quantity taken may be reduced but the pricing system will only allocate efficiently if each consumer is required to pay the marginal cost of each unit of water consumed. This point has been developed in detail in Chapter 2, pages 15-26. If a marginal cost pricing procedure is used each firm will abstract water until the marginal value in use of the last unit is equal to the price charged (i.e. the marginal cost). At this point no re-allocation of water between consumers could occur that would cause a net increase in benefit to society. This, in fact, would be an equilibrium position where the quantity demanded at that price was equal to the quantity taken and supplied.

To return to a consideration of the chemical firms alone, it was found that tonnage of raw materials was the only independent variable that produced a high enough level of explanation to be used for predictive purposes. The number of persons employed, and the price paid for metered water supplies were both significantly related to water consumption, but the $R^2$ values and the standard error of the residuals precluded their use in forecasting.

b The food manufacturing industry (pp 75-79).
In this industry group the tonnage of raw materials entering the manufacturing process was also found to be the best explanatory variable of water consumption. A simple regression equation $Q^2 = a + bT$ explained 86.7% of the variation between firms in the quantity of water *purchased*. This same equation form also accounted for 90.7% of the variation in the level of *private abstraction*.

With these high $R^2$ values it is possible to calculate a firm's water demands with a relatively high degree of accuracy. For example, if a food manufacturer wanted to establish a new plant, capable of handling 75,000 tons of raw materials per annum,[5] then that plant is likely to demand approximately 78 mgy of water from the local water undertaking,[6] *and* a further 239 mgy from a privately owned water source.[7] The constant term of the regression equation $QA^2 = a + bT$ suggests that food manufacturers only find it worthwhile to *abstract* water privately when over approximately 120 mgy are required. As has already been discussed, the actual quantity of water which a firm will be able to abstract from private sources will depend on the resource allocation procedure finally introduced by the river authorities. It should

also be mentioned that any non-fulfilment of a firm's abstraction demands
may result in an increased demand for water supplied by the local
undertakings. Needless to say this means that any forecasts of water
purchases may understate the true position. Although no price cross-effect[8]
between purchased and abstracted water was observable, it is probable
that some substitution will occur when firms are refused permission to
abstract or to increase abstraction from private sources of water. In other
words substitution may be induced by absolute stringency rather than
by price increases.

The number of persons employed was a second variable that was
significantly related to the quantities of water purchased and privately
abstracted by food manufacturers. A multiple regression equation with
ton-input and employment as the independent variables could not be
used as a forecasting model because multicollinearity distorts the
regression parameters. In the case of *purchased* supplies the $R^2$ value of
0.724 (72.4%) is high enough to enable the equation $Q = a + bE$ to be
used in forecasting. Estimation errors are likely to be higher if the
employment equation is used as the level of explanation is lower than
that obtained from the ton-input equation. Despite this it may well
be useful in verifying the forecasts derived from $Q^2 = a + bT$. In addition,
there may well be some firms that are unable to estimate the tonnage of
raw materials that will be used when full capacity output is reached, but
are able to give an approximate employment figure. It has been estimated
that a mean-sized food manufacturing firm, employing 500 persons, will
demand approximately 64 mgy of water from the local undertaking.[9]
This figure is close to the value of 78 mgy which was estimated as the
probable consumption of a firm handling the mean tonnage of raw
materials. Although there is no guarantee that a firm employing the mean
number of persons will also handle the mean quantity of raw materials,
it is known that these two variables are positively and linearly related.
It is believed that the fact that these two quantity estimates are similar
in magnitude increases confidence in the forecasting equations.

c The drink manufacturing industry (pp 79-82).
The regression results for this industry group were such that forecasts
can only be made for the quantity of water *privately abstracted*; $R^2$
values in the purchased water regressions were well below those needed
for forecasting. As has been discussed previously the results obtained
for this industry group will be subject to much error due to the very
low response rate in the sample survey. Any forecasts based on these

results are also likely to be subject to large degrees of error. In particular
it is probable that the demand for privately abstracted water will be
under-estimated due to the consistent non-response of large private
abstractors.[10] The value of any forecasts is made even more debatable
by the fact that the regression coefficient of the best-fit equation proved
to be negative. This implies that the level of abstraction declines as the
quantity of raw materials used increases. In fact the regression parameters
suggest that a firm using over 93,000 tons of raw materials will not
abstract any water from private sources of supply,[11] which is not likely
to be a realistic forecast.

d The paper and paper products industry (pp 82-87).
Very few of the significant relationships established for this industry
group can be used for forecasting purposes, as the levels of explanation
derived from the best-fit regression equations are normally well below
the cut-off value of 60%. This is shown in column 8, table 13 page 83.
No forecasts can be attempted for the quantity of water that will be
demanded from local undertakings. It is, however, possible to make
some tentative statements concerning the possible desired level of
*private abstraction*: the actual quantity abstracted will depend on
the decisions of river authorities.

When attempting to forecast the amount of *private abstraction* that
a firm will wish to undertake, two equation forms $QA = a + bT$ and
$QA = a + bT + cD$ can be used. The second equation should give a rather
more accurate result, and has the advantage that it differentiates between
raw paper and paper product manufacturers. Irrespective of the type of
manufacturing process, a firm in the paper industry is unlikely to wish to
abstract water from a private source unless over 200 mgy are required.
This figure is obtained from the constant term in the regression equation.
If a firm in the paper industry planned to establish a branch plant, which
would be able to handle 50,000 tons of raw materials (this is
approximately the mean size of the surveyed concerns) it is likely that
it would apply to abstract approximately 1200 mgy.[12] This figure was
calculated from the equation $QA = a + bT$ and so no distinction between
paper product and raw paper producers is made. If the plant were to
produce raw paper the above figure would in all probability underestimate
the true level of demand, and a more accurate estimate can be obtained
from the equation which incorporates the dummy variable. It was found
that a *raw paper producer*, handling 50,000 tons of raw materials, would
probably wish to take over 1,500 mgy from private sources.[13] On the

other hand a *paper product firm* using the same quantity of raw materials would only demand 600 mgy.[14] This latter case is, however, unlikely to occur in practice as product manufacturers rarely use over 12,000 tons of raw materials, and below this level of input private abstraction is unlikely to be worthwhile.

e Metal and metal product manufacturers (pp 90-91).
The title of this industry group is rather a misleading one since primary metal manufacturers are under-represented in the south east; only one such firm is included within the respondents. Any forecasts for this group are, therefore, only strictly applicable to metal product firms, and not to those engaged in the large-scale primary processing of metals.

Tonnage of raw materials entering the manufacturing process was used as the forecasting variable in all the industry groups discussed to date. In the metals group, however, the number of persons employed was most closely correlated to the demand for water, and high levels of explanation were produced by the best-fit equation forms. No significant relationships could be established between tonnage of inputs and the quantity of water used.

As the best-fit equation form $Q = a + bE^2$ yielded an $R^2$ value of 0.96 (96%) it can be used with a high degree of confidence to forecast the probable demand for water *purchased* from local undertakings. Supposing a metal product plant was being constructed which had a full capacity employment level of 400 persons;[15] then it would be likely to demand approximately 5 mgy from its local water undertaking.[16] The positive constant term in the equation implies that no metal manufacturing plant will be constructed that does not demand approximately 570,000 gallons of water from the local undertakings per annum. Presumably plants requiring less than this quantity would not be economically viable units. It is, however, possible that the sample bias towards plants employing over 15 persons has contributed to this positive threshold level of water consumption.

Employment figures can also be used to forecast the quantity of water that a metal product producer is likely to wish to *abstract* from private sources of supply. The results will, however, be subject to larger errors than those for the quantity of water purchased because relatively few of these firms find private abstraction worthwhile. In the first place the firm must employ over approximately 200 persons before it will consider private abstraction to be an economic proposition. Smaller firms will satisfy all their water demands by purchasing supplies from local water undertakings. Larger metal firms may own a private water supply source but even they will take relatively small quantities. For example, the firm employing 400 persons is likely to take under half a million gallons of water per annum.[17]

f Non metallic mineral manufacturers (pp 91-94).
Although some of the independent variables were significantly related to the water demand of firms in this industry group, by and large the levels of explanation were low. This is most probably due to the polyglot nature of the firms within the group. Forecasts can only be attempted for the quantity of water that may be *purchased* from the water supply industry, and even here the standard error of the residuals indicates that the forecast errors may well be large (as high as 50% error either side of the forecast). Confidence in the accuracy of the forecasts must, therefore, be very low. Using the best-fit equation form $Q = a + bE^2$ it was found that a mean sized firm employing 140 persons, would possibly demand 2.5 million gallons of water from the local water undertaking. It was also found that no non-metallic minerals firm is likely to demand less than 150,000 gallons per annum, irrespective of the size of its labour force.

g 'Other manufacturers'[18] (pp 96-99).
As expected the water demands of firms in these labour intensive manufacturing groups were most closely associated with the number of persons employed. Most of these firms obtain all their water requirements by *purchase* and so forecasts can not be made of the quantity of water *abstracted privately*. As very few of these firms use water for cooling and processing the water purchases are relatively small. A mean sized firm, employing 180 persons, would on average only demand approximately 600,000 gallons of water per annum from the local undertaking.[19] Similarly a firm using the mean quantity of raw material inputs (6000 tons) would demand approximately 520,000 gallons per annum.[20] It can be seen that the quantities of water demanded by the firms employing the mean tonnage and the mean number of persons are similar in magnitude. This was also the case in the food industry and as there it is believed that the similarity in the values increases confidence in the forecasting equations.

*3 The demand forecasts: summary and implications.*
In the previously discussed industry groups it has been possible to estimate the quantitative effects on a firm's water consumption of changes in either

the number of persons employed, or the level of raw materials used. Numerical values can only be assigned to the change in the demand for water which results from a variation in one of the independent explanatory variables when the regression equation produced an $R^2$ value of over 0.60 (60%). Below this level of explanation the degree of probable error would be too large to produce meaningful forecasts. Using the 60% figure as a cut-off value it was possible to measure the effects of a change in the level of ton-input on the demand for *purchased* water by chemical, food and 'other' firms. Likewise some tentative measurements were made of the possible changes in the level of *private abstraction* undertaken by chemicals, food and paper manufacturers resulting from variations in the quantity of raw materials used. The effects of increases or decreases in the number of persons employed on the demand for *purchased* water can be stated quantitatively for the food, metals, non-metallic minerals, and 'other' groups, while the impact of such variations in the labour force on the level of *private abstraction* can only be measured for metal firms.

It must, however, be stressed that the use of the regression statistics[21] in quantitative forecasting is subject to certain limitations. In the first instance the analysis is strictly applicable only to the study area in which the sample survey was taken. There is no certainty that the established regression coefficients will be the same in all other areas of the country. Although it is probable that the same variables will be related to the demand for water, the exact nature of the relationship may vary. This variation may be due to the changing composition of an industry group; for example it is known that primary metal manufacture is under-represented in the study area. A second limitation in the use of the estimated coefficients is that the regression line is only a fitted average and individual firms may be well away from this line.[22] Thirdly, it is possibly that the regression statistics are biassed due to selective non-response to the 'Industrial Survey'. This bias is known to have a serious effect on the results for drink manufacturers[23] but in the other industry groups there is no evidence that the non-respondents differ significantly in character from the respondents. The whole survey was, however, deliberately biassed towards the larger manufacturing units; all firms employing less than 15 persons were excluded from the sample frame, and in addition multi-plant firms were only required to supply details for their largest productive unit. All these limitations must be taken into account in the application of the regression statistics.

Although quantitative forecasts can only be made when the regression equation relating two variables produces a level of explanation greater than

60% ($R^2$ = 0.60), it is possible to state in qualitative terms the probable reaction of the dependent variable to changes in the explanatory variables whenever significant relationships have been established. These qualitative, or directional, forecasts are not subject to many of the same limitations as the numerical forecasts. In the first place sample bias may affect the value of the regression coefficients but it is unlikely to affect the sign of the observed relationships. Likewise variations in the composition of the industry groups probably will not be great enough to alter the sign of the coefficients or to affect the general shape of the best-fit regression line. It is also thought that the same relative positions of the industry groups will be maintained. For example, the addition of one employee will probably cause the demand for purchased water to increase approximately 60 times faster in the food industry than in the chemical industry.[24]

Many of the qualitative statements that can be made are rather obvious ones. For example, an increase in the tonnage of raw materials used or in the number of persons employed by a firm will be associated with an increased demand for both purchased and privately abstracted supplies of water. By comparing the relative effects of changes in these inputs it is possible to distinguish those industries whose growth is likely to impose the greatest strain on local water resources. It is known that an increase in the number of persons employed in food and paper firms would increase the demand for purchased water by much greater quantities than would equivalent employment increases in the chemical, metal, non-metal minerals, engineering or 'other' groups.[25] Likewise it is known that an increase in the tonnage of raw materials used will have a much greater impact on the quantity of water demanded from *private abstraction sources* by the larger chemical and raw paper producers than it will on that demanded by food, metal product and non-metallic mineral manufacturers. In both of the former groups an increase of 1000 tons in the quantity of raw materials used is associated with an increase in demand for abstracted water of over 25 mgy, whereas a similar tonnage rise is associated with demand increases of less than 3 mgy in the other groups. This comparative information should be useful both in planning regional industrial development, and in planning the allocation of water resources between areas. Rather more capital will need to be invested in expanding the water supplies of areas with a high proportion of firms whose demands increase rapidly with rising levels of employment and raw material inputs.

Qualitative forecasting is perhaps of greatest importance when the impact of price changes on the demand for *purchased supplies of water* is considered. In no industry group was the level of explanation derived from the regression of price on quantity sufficiently high to allow numerical precision in forecasting from the equation. But for some industry groups significant relationships were established between these two variables. Therefore, the degree of responsiveness of demand to price changes can be considered. When the quantity of water taken by all firms was regressed on the price paid for metered supplies of water it was found that demand was *price elastic* at the mean price paid for 1000 gallons of water. In other words, all things being equal, a price increase would result in a more than proportionate decline in the demand for metered water. Therefore, the price mechanism should be an effective method of rationing scarce supplies of the resource. If price increases took place at the same time as a growth in employment or in the tonnage of raw materials entering the manufacturing process, then it is unlikely that an absolute decline in the quantity demanded would occur, as shifts in the demand curve would offset the movement along the curve caused by price changes. (See Figure 14.)

**Figure 14 A shift in the demand curve for water**

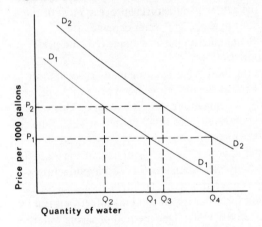

When price is set at $P_1$, $Q_1$ gallons of water is demanded. All things being equal a price increase to $P_2$ will result in a decrease of demand to $Q_2$. But if an increase in the level of employment causes the demand curve to shift outwards then $Q_3$ will be demanded. This still represents a relative decrease in demand as $Q_4$ gallons would have been taken if no price rise had occurred.

This implies that a general increase in the price charged per 1000 gallons by water undertakings in the 'study' area would result in at least a falling off in the rate of increase in the demand for water from manufacturing industry. The result of price rises should be a saving of water, but a *decrease* in the revenue of the water undertakings. Conversely a price reduction would increase demand and should also increase the total revenue of undertakings. General price increases therefore would be most effective when an undertaking has no spare supply capacity, whereas price decreases could be used during off-peak periods to utilize spare capacity and to increase revenue. This could argue for lower prices to be charged to manufacturers during the winter months, although the price elasticity may alter over the seasons.

The overall picture does, however, disguise quite wide differences between the industry groups in the degree of responsiveness to price changes. In four of the industry groups, metals, plastics, engineering and 'other', no significant relationship between price paid and the quantity taken was in evidence. Price of metered water is a secondary or minor factor in the determination of the quantity of water purchased. As has been mentioned earlier, most of the firms in these industry groups use only small quantities of water in the actual manufacturing process; most of the water demanded is used for staff hygiene. The water demands are, therefore, closely related to the number of persons employed, and price changes are of negligible importance.

It was found that firms in the food manufacturing industry were most responsive to price changes. Even at the lowest recorded price of 25 pence per 1000 gallons the elasticity of demand for water was over 3. This value increased to 6.7 at the highest observed price of 49 pence per 1000 gallons. As the relationship between the metered price of water and the amount purchased from the local water undertakings was significant at the 99.95% level of probability these elasticity measurements for food manufacturers can be taken with a high degree of confidence. The implication that arises from the highly elastic demand for water is that food manufacturers can substitute capital for water relatively easily. One method of saving water, which is commonly used in modern food factories is the successive re-use of water for progressively dirtier jobs. For example, in the production of canned vegetables potable water is used to cook the product; this is then recirculated to wash the peeled vegetables; from there it could be used to wash the food during peeling, and finally to wash the fresh vegetables before peeling, only after all these stages will the water be discarded.[26] This procedure brings about a considerable saving of water but it does involve rather more capital investment. In addition the plant must be laid out in the appropriate sequence to avoid the unnecessary recycling of water.

Demand for water also proved to be highly elastic for firms in the non-metallic minerals group. At the lowest price paid per 1000 gallons the elasticity was 2.5, and this increased as the price rose. Once again this high degree of responsiveness to price implies that other factors of production can be substituted for water with relative ease. It could also imply that high prices provide a greater incentive to avoid wastage. Both drink manufacturers and paper firms had elastic demands for water at all the observed prices of water, but these elasticities were lower (between 1 and 3) than those estimated for the food and non-metallic mineral firms. Chemical producers proved to be least responsive to price changes. The demand curve for water of this industry group only became elastic at prices of 33 pence and over. This implies that the substitution of capital for water is relatively costly and will only become worthwhile at the higher price levels.

Both the variables used for *quantitative* forecasting (tonnage of raw materials and the number of persons employed) are closely linked to the firm's productive capacity and output. As these variables are also closely related to the level of industrial water consumption, it can be argued that attempts to curb the quantity of water used may result in the relative or even absolute decline of manufacturing output. The validity of this argument will partly depend upon the degree of slack that exists in industrial water usage. In other words, if water is being used wastefully and this waste could be removed without imposing additional costs, then the restriction of water supplies would not have an impact on the firm's productive capacity. Similarly, if the firm is able to substitute other factors of production, for example capital, for water without materially increasing total costs, then productivity will not be affected. On the other hand, if factor substitution is difficult or costly any attempts to decrease water consumption must be reflected in increasing costs and this could result in a decline in the firm's output. An increase in costs may shift the supply curve for each firm's product to the left; at each market price the firm is prepared to produce less output as production costs are higher. From the price elasticity measures discussed previously it appears that firms in the food, drink, non-metallic minerals and paper industries can substitute other factors of production for purchased supplies of water with relative ease. In these cases total (or marginal) production costs should not be greatly increased when the availability of metered water is reduced, or when the price is increased. Cost increases will be greater in industry groups where purchased water has no economic substitute. But even in these groups water costs usually account for a very small proportion of total costs and so productive output should not be affected greatly.

It is, however, more difficult to judge whether a reduction in the availability of water for *private abstraction* can take place without increasing costs and decreasing productivity. In the regression analysis no relationships could be established between the cost of abstraction and the quantity taken. This probably is the result of the exceptionally low cost per 1000 gallons. From the 'Industrial Survey' questionnaire it would appear that large price increases would result in water being recycled. This is especially the case for drink, paper, chemical and mechanical engineering concerns. The recycling of process water often does require considerable capital investment, although it is normally spread over 20 or more years. In some firms a reduction in water usage may only be possible in the long-run as it would involve the large-scale reorganization of the plant and its water using equipment. Any savings of water resulting from attempts to restrict private abstraction must be balanced against any cost increases experienced by each firm.

It has been suggested that the greatest cost increases occur when a reduction in the availability of water for effluent dilution occurs.[27] This is particularly important when a firm can only reduce the quantity or change the quality of the effluent by altering the actual manufacturing process. It was found that the 1951 and 1961 *River Acts* have already resulted in increased waste disposal costs for many firms. All leather producers have experienced an increase, as have over 50% of the food, drink, paper, and chemical firms which responded to the sample survey. In the leather, chemicals and paper industries process changes have commonly to be introduced to change the nature of the effluent.

In Chapter 2 it was asserted that there is no physical shortage of water; the problem is an economic one of allocating the resource between competitive uses. Before water supplies are restricted the true costs involved must be known and compared with the costs involved in expanding available supplies. To take an extreme and hypothetical example, if the existing withdrawals from one stream course reduced the water level below the 'minimum acceptable flow' then any new plant, or an expanding firm would probably be refused an abstraction licence. Yet the costs to these firms, and therefore to society, of finding alternative methods of production, alternative water sources, or even alternative locations, may be greater and possibly far greater than the cost of supplementing the stream flow. The major problem, however, is that of finding the real costs imposed on the affected firms. Many firms are unwilling to divulge detailed cost information. Others are unable to give the required data because no separate accounts are kept. In addition, some of the real costs of the restriction are external to the firm as relative or even absolute decreases in the productivity of one manufacturing unit have repercussions on other producers.

**Rates of growth in industrial water consumption**
The demand forecasts based on the quantity regression analysis can only be projected into the future if it is assumed that the functional relationships between the independent variables and the quantity of water taken have not changed over time. This limitation is less important when the time rates of growth given by the firms themselves are taken, although even here it must still be assumed that no major change will occur in the basis on which these forecasts were derived. Forecasts are most reliable when time trend data are obtainable for the dependent variable (in this case the demand for water) and for the independent explanatory variables. Unfortunately, such data are not available, therefore the only method of obtaining information over a time-scale was to ask the sampled firms to estimate the past and possible future rates of growth of their water consumption. While it is acknowledged that such estimates are inevitably subject to error they can at least be used as a guide. The growth rates given for past consumption should be relatively accurate, but the possible future increases in consumption must be treated with caution.

All firms which answered the second part of the 'Industrial Survey' questionnaire gave the average percentage change that had occurred in their annual water usage over a period of 10 years (i.e. from 1955-1965). As each manufacturer also supplied data on the total quantity of water taken during 1965, it was possible to calculate the average annual increase in the gallonage of water used by each firm. By adding up these total consumption figures and the average annual increase figures it was possible to calculate the annual consumption and the annual increase in consumption for each industry group, as well as for all the sampled firms. From these actual gallonages the average annual growth rates were calculated (see table 25).

It was found that the water usage of all the *sampled* firms showed a net average increase of 1.8% per annum between 1955 and 1965. This does not imply that industrial water consumption in south east England increased at this rate. When the sample survey was taken a variable sampling fraction was used (89 p. 84). In other words more manufacturers were sampled in

**Table 25. Water consumption growth rates**

| industry group | average annual growth rate. 1955-65 | estimated future annual growth rate |
|---|---|---|
| A food | 0.82% | 2.72% |
| B drink | 3.64% | 3.22% |
| C paper and paper products | 1.88% | 0.30% |
| D plastics and rubber | 0.97% | 0.71% |
| E chemicals | 1.41% | 0.36% |
| F non-metallic minerals | 4.77% | 0.88% |
| G metals and metal products | 3.63% | 1.70% |
| H mechanical engineering | 7.95% | 7.89% |
| I precision engineering | 0.68% | 0.39% |
| J other | 8.70% | 0.93% |
| K all sampled firms | 1.79% | 0.53% |
| L weighted total for firms in south east england | 2.03% | 0.79% |

those industry groups containing firms with widely disparate water using characteristics. (Chapter 1, pages 4-5.) This means that such groups occupy a more important position in the sample than they do in the industrial structure of south east England. To obtain an estimate for the growth of total industrial consumption in the 'study area' it was necessary to normalise the data. This was done by weighting the figures obtained for each industry group to arrive at the overall population proportions. This weighting procedure also corrected any bias in the results caused by a variation between industry groups in the response rate to the 'Industrial Survey' questionnaire, as the weights needed were calculated from the number of respondents in each industry group.

As a result of the weighting it is estimated that total industrial water usage increased by an average of 2% per annum over the years 1955-65. This increase includes both water purchased from local water undertakings and that obtained from private abstraction. This value is only slightly lower than that estimated by the Sub-Committee on the Growing Demand for Water for the same time period (1955-65). On behalf of the Sub-Committee

. . . the Federation of British Industries approached the trade associations of six industries which, together with the nationalized industries, were believed to account for a substantial part of the industrial demand for water. The industries selected were brewing, chemicals, iron and steel, leather, paper-making and textiles (124. (a). p. 4).

Only two industries made any attempt to forecast the future demand for water, and on this very meagre information the Sub-Committee predicted that industrial demand for water from private abstraction sources would increase by 25% in England and Wales over the 10 year period, 1955-65. In addition an increase of 23% was envisaged in the demand for water from the public water suppliers. The Sub-Committee never intended these figures to be anything but working measures, but it is disturbing to find the growth rates have been uaed to plan the future development of water supply sources. As even small annual overestimates assume large proportions over the years it is important that extrapolated estimates are based on adequate surveys.

In 1965, the Water Resources Board set up a Technical Committee to consider the water supply situation in south east England (127). In their report the Technical Committee used the sub-committee's growth figures to obtain an estimate for the quantity of water taken by industry from private sources in 1965. From this present usage figure the Technical Committee went on to estimate demand up to the year 2001. These assessments of future demand were based on an assumed growth rate of 4% per annum (127. pp. 15-6). The only apparent basis for the use of this particular rate is that it was the one adopted by the National Economic Development Council for the expansion of national productivity. Even if this rate of growth in national productivity is achieved there is no reason why net water consumption in the south east should increase at the same rate, much will depend on which areas and industries undergo the greatest expansion.

The selection of a 4% growth rate also seems to ignore the fact that the licensing of abstractions introduced by the 1963 *Water Resources Act* and the charging system which will be put into operation shortly should alter the demand for water from private sources. From the 'Industrial Survey' questionnaire (question 4. Section B) it was found that 80% of firms using private water supplies had either been refused permission to increase their consumption (8%) or felt that the licensing scheme would cause an absolute or relative decline in their future water usage. This opinion is clearly reflected in the firms' estimates of their future water consumption growth rates. On average the sampled firms expect an annual increase in their future water consumption of only 0.53%. As table 25 shows, when the above figure was weighted to obtain a value representative for all manufacturers in the 'study' area the average expected increase rose to 0.79% per annum. This does not mean that industrial demand for water will only increase by this percentage as it only refers to those firms already established and takes no account of the demands from manufacturers not yet established in the area. In part the very low expected growth rate may be a result of the firms' inability to project their demands into the future; predictions of technological innovations can rarely be attempted. It was, however, apparent from the test interviews (see Chapter 1 page 5) that many manufacturers had concrete reasons for expecting at least a falling off in their rate of increase in water consumption. Most papermakers, for example, were convinced that the new regulation of private abstraction would cause a decline in their gross water usage. This is of considerable importance as raw paper producers account for approximately 65% of all water abstracted by the sampled firms. Some furniture manufacturers were also expecting a lower future rate of increase, as the past increase had been unusually high due to the introduction of water wash spray booths. (see below).

The discussion so far has been concerned with the overall growth rates for all firms, but there are some striking differences between industry groups both in actual past and expected future rates of increase in water usage (table 25 page 150). It appears that food manufacturers and precision engineers have experienced the lowest average increases over the last 10 years. Many food firms in fact reported a net decrease in usage due to the introduction of the systematic re-use of water for progressively dirtier jobs. (The point has been discussed earlier on page 146.) This factor has probably been the chief cause of the very low average annual growth rate of 0.82% p.a. In the precision engineering group many firms have experienced a stable consumption of water over the ten year period 1955 to 1965 and this accounts for the low overall growth rate of 0.68% per annum. At the other end of the scale mechanical engineers and 'other' manufacturers appear to have experienced average annual increases in water usage of 7.95% and 8.7% respectively. It must, however, be pointed out that in both these industries the increase takes place on a relatively small total consumption, and therefore the gallonages of water involved are not great. Much of the increase experienced in the 'other' group is accounted for by the already mentioned high growth rate amongst the furniture manufacturers. In this industry, one of the wood finishing processes involves the removal of excess cellulose lacquer. Today, this is commonly done in water wash spray booths, and the effluent is collected at the bottom of the booths. The older, alternative method is to use dry backed booths but in this case effluent is released to the air, and may result in severe air pollution. When water wash booths are installed a large, but once and for all, increase in water consumption takes place.[28] The reasons for the high rate of growth in the quantity of water taken by mechanical

engineers are rather more difficult to assess. In part at least the value is
inflated by the very large increases experienced by one firm relocating in
the study area in 1961. But this does not explain why these firms expect
to increase consumption by over 7% in the future.

By and large the predicted future rates of growth in consumption are
lower than those actually experienced over the past ten years. The only
group to which this does not apply is the food manufacturing industry.
From the test interviews it would appear that most sampled food producers
already practise considerable recycling and re-use of water, and, as they
are unable to foresee future technical innovations in water saving
equipment, they feel that water usage will increase as output rises. The large
decline in the annual rate of growth in water consumption predicted by
'other' manufacturers stems simply from the fact that most furniture
producers now use water wash booths.

Most firms that abstract water from privately owned sources have
indicated that they expect their future annual increase in withdrawals to
be low. For example, paper firms only anticipate an average net increase in
total water usage of 0.3% per annum, compared with the 1.9% experienced
over the last ten years. This decrease represents a considerable gallonage of
water since these firms use large quantities for processing, cooling and
effluent disposal. Similarly, non-metallic mineral producers only expect a
future increase of 0.9% per annum compared with the past rate of 4.8%. It
is possible, however, that predicted increases in some industry groups may
well underestimate the actual rise, especially if new water using processes
are introduced. On the other hand, it is thought that the future expansion
of industrial water consumption may well be curtailed because any
increase in private abstraction will depend on the policy decisions of river
authorities. The capital investment decisions of firms will be influenced by
their *expectations* concerning the future availability of water. As most
manufacturers do not expect to be able to increase their withdrawals from
private sources, some of them may well be induced to install recycling or
other water saving equipment now. In this way expectations may cause an
actual reduction in future demands.

The question of how much water industry will require in the year 2001
is largely meaningless and attempts to answer it on the basis of past
consumption patterns, or on the basis of expected increases in industrial
productivity will probably lead to misleading results. A rather more
relevant question would be 'how much water will manufacturing industry
demand if a charge of 3d., 6d. or 1/- was placed on each 1000 gallons
abstracted?' Unfortunately, the quantity regression analysis was not

successful in providing an answer to this, as no relationship could be established between the level of private abstraction and the cost of abstraction. This was, however, largely due to the fact that the cost of each 1000 gallons taken is minimal and also some firms are unable to distinguish between abstraction costs and other general running expenses of the factory. From the 'Industrial Survey'(question B.12) it would appear that a price/cost increase of 100%[29] would greatly increase the amount of recycling. Over 50% of firms in the drink, paper and mechanical engineering industries claim that such a price rise would force them to install recycling equipment; similar claims are also made by over 40% of chemical and furniture firms. In addition a number of manufacturers say that they would be encouraged to make changes in their process to decrease water consumption; for example, 40% of mechanical engineers, 40% of furniture manufacturers, 20% of chemical producers, 18.2% of the paper firms and 12.5% of drink makers.

Another relevant question would be 'how much can be made available to manufacturing industry if the stream courses are allocated up to the "minimum acceptable flow"?' It must be borne in mind that the cost of maintaining this minimum flow is the opportunity cost of water in all the other uses, including effluent disposal.[30] Once water availability has been estimated the problem then arises of how to allocate it between competing uses. As has already been discussed in Chapter two (page 23) an economically efficient allocation is not achieved by allowing the first applicants to have all the water they require, while refusing to give any supply to newly established concerns. Ideally, the water should be rationed by the price mechanism. The firm with an inelastic demand for privately abstracted water, usually one for which the substitution of capital for water is either impossible or too costly, will bid a higher price for the water than firms for which substitutes are available. When some measure is obtained of the price manufacturers would be willing to pay for various quantities of water, it should be possible to determine the level to which existing water resources should be supplemented.

## Water supply and industrial location

The role of water as a factor in industrial location was analysed in detail in Chapter 5. It remains to discuss here the possible future influence that the availability of water supply and effluent disposal facilities will have on the regional development of manufacturing industry, and on the locational decisions of individual firms. During this discussion the probable effects of

water resource planning on the location of manufacturers will also be
considered.

## 1 Water supply and regional development

There is no evidence that past variations in the price or availability of
water supplies have played any part in the differential rates of regional
development. Nor is it likely that any noticeable variations in the
distribution of different types of manufacturing industry between regions
have been produced by diverse water supply conditions. Hitherto water
has been readily available in all regions and little if any regional differences
occurred in either the price paid for purchased supplies, or the costs of
private abstraction. Once a firm had chosen to locate within any particular
area (see Chapter 5, p. 105) there was almost invariably a site with suitable
water supply and effluent facilities within the area of search. It was
suggested in the previous chapter, however, that the intra-regional
distribution of different types of producers may well have been affected
by the availability of water supplies. A firm, requiring water in quantities
above that economically purchased from local undertakings, has to locate
to a suitable source of private abstraction water. Thus in the south east
there are discernible clusters of large water users (such as paper producers
and public utilities) along water courses and above water bearing strata,
which are situated in close proximity to urban areas.

In the long-run future the availability of water may become more
important in the regional distribution, and the regional growth, of the
various manufacturing industries. The influence of water may be exercised
through four separate media:—

a   The Board of Trade location advisory service could attempt to steer
large water users away from regions with a shortage of available water. This
could be made highly effective as the Board is responsible for the issue or
refusal of Industrial Development Certificates, without which
manufacturers are unable to build new plants or rebuild existing ones.

b   Local councils may refuse planning permission for the location or
expansion of firms using large gallonages of water or producing large
amounts of trade effluent. As was seen earlier it appears that this source of
influence has already been exercised in southern Essex and in the Lea
Valley area of Hertfordshire. (Chapter 5, p. 106.)

c   The regional location of firms relying on purchased supplies of water
may be influenced by the refusal of certain local water undertakings to
give a supply, as they are entitled to do under Section 27 of the 1945
*Water Act*. Such refusals would probably only occur when the industrial

demands would strain the developed supply capacity of the undertakings. The attitude of the suppliers is understandable as their first duty in law is to serve domestic consumers. Rather less understandable is the apparent reluctance of *some* authorities to extend their supply capacity even when the firm is prepared to pay the long-run marginal cost of its water.[31] Although this situation may be rare it is claimed that it has occurred twice in one large water authority in the Midlands,[32] and undoubtedly has arisen in some of the smaller undertakings.

d  Perhaps the most important bodies affecting the location of large water users will be the river authorities. They not only have the power to issue or refuse abstraction licences, but also by 1st April 1969 they must impose a charge on each 1000 gallons of water abstracted privately (119. p. 63). It is possible that some firms will be forced to migrate to regions where water is in surplus supply, or where the gallonage charge is low.

It is likely, however, that any changes in the regional distribution and growth of manufacturing industries will only become apparent in the very long-run. In the first place the planning bodies can only really influence the location of newly established firms, or those wishing to relocate their plant, or part of their plant; such firms only account for a very small proportion of the country's productive capacity. The river authorities, through the new per unit charge imposed on private abstractors, are the only bodies able to influence the location of established, non-expanding firms; but it is suggested that regional differences in the charge per 1000 gallons would have to be very great to justify the expense of a firm relocating elsewhere.

Secondly, the regional distribution of industry will only be altered by these attempts to conserve water if abstraction licences or planning permissions were refused over the whole of certain regions, in which case the firms concerned would have to seek sites outside their areas of origin or outside the area preferred for economic reasons. If the expansion of industrial water consumption was only curtailed in parts of a region it is probable that the affected firms would search for an alternative location within the same region. In this case the overall regional distribution of industry would be left unaffected.

This does not, of course, mean that the regulation and pricing of water withdrawals has little effect on the activities of individual firms, but rarely will a firm be so critically affected that it will seek an alternative location immediately. Only two of the sampled firms, both in the chemical industry, claimed that a 100% increase in the price of water would make them consider relocating to an area of cheaper supplies. In general the

expenses involved in rebuilding elsewhere, in writing off existing
equipment and buildings, and in retraining labour will far outweigh the
cost of introducing water saving equipment designed to maintain the
existing level of consumption, or the cost of paying any price increase in
full. It has been shown by White (136. p. 463), Sporck (107) and others
that manufacturing industry is capable of adapting the level of water usage
to suit a range of prices and levels of availability. The possibility does exist,
however, that the refusal of additional water supplies may encourage firms
to establish a branch plant elsewhere. For example, a rather similar
situation arose when some of the wells owned by Thames Board Limited,
Purfleet, Essex, became saline and reduced the firms effective supply of
water. The company has not relocated the parent plant but a branch
producing high quality products has been established elsewhere.

One important aspect of the control of industrial location through the
withholding of planning permission or through the refusal to allow private
abstraction is that the firms concerned are faced with an absolute non-
availability of water. Existing firms holding licences of right are able to use
as much water as they were using before 1963, even if this includes an
element of waste. On the other hand the new firms may not be allowed
any supply even if they are prepared to pay highly for it, and could use it
in a highly productive way. As has been suggested earlier (see Chapter 2,
p. 23) a licensing system based on 'first come, first served' is an extremely
inefficient way of rationing a scarce resource. The newer firm is not
allowed to choose between an area with high water costs but low total
production costs, and one with low water charges but with less favourable
production conditions. Thus the overall costs of some firms may be
inflated vis-à-vis those of other producers; this will be reflected in the
prices for their products and may result in the cumulative misallocation of
resources in the economy.

One further point, however, is that if the water authorities continue to
follow current policy and extend supplies to cover all foreseeable 'needs or
requirements', then there will be no long term shortage of available water
and therefore no long term effect on the regional distribution of industry.
There seems in fact to be little relationship between the introduction of
licensing to conserve water and the methods used by the water industry
to calculate future water consumption.

*2 Water supply and an individual firm's locational decisions*
As was argued in Chapter 5, the factors which influence the regional
distribution and growth of industry need not be the same as those

influencing an individual firm when its locational decision is made. It remains here to consider whether the availability of water supply and effluent disposal facilities is likely to play a more important part in locational decision-making in the future than it has in the past.

It was found that for most of the sampled manufacturers the availability of water supply or effluent disposal facilities was not a critical factor in their actual location decision; less than 10% of the firms ranked water in places 1 or 2. There was also no evidence that water would be placed any higher if the sample firms were to seek new locations now: no significant difference emerged between the number of firms giving water a high rank in the past and the number which would rank it highly in the hypothetical present decision. This feature is perhaps rather surprising as the licensing of abstractions introduced in 1963 could have been expected to cause a relative increase in the importance of water as a location factor, at least for those firms requiring a private abstraction source. Even in the paper, food and plastics groups, where a high proportion of manufacturers abstract from privately owned sources, there was no significant increase in the ranks given to the factor.

When the sampled firms were formed into sub-groups based on the number of persons employed it was found that firms with over 1000 employees gave water a much more important position in their locational decisions than did the smaller firms. It is tempting to conclude from this that as the average size of manufacturing concerns increases over time so will the importance of the water factor. This conclusion does, however, involve the assumption that the same functional relationship between the variables will exist over time (see Chapter 6, pp. 133-134). Despite this limitation it would be fair to say that large firms requiring privately abstracted water are likely to find their choice of possible sites restricted by the availability of water.

It would appear from the analysis of the rankings given to water by firms of different ages that the availability of a suitable water supply was most important in the locational decisions of firms established before 1850. Since then the relative importance of water has declined steadily (see table 23) as the public water supply industry has extended its network, and has become increasingly willing to supply industrial consumers. This does not mean that water is now an unconsidered factor in location decisions, but only that finding a suitable water supply is much less difficult than satisfying demands for the other factors of production. If the public water industry continues to supply manufacturers, and if new water resources are developed there will be no tendency for the availability of water supply to gain in relative importance in a firm's decision making.

When asked whether water will become a more important location factor, many firms felt that it would (see table 26). This was especially

Table 26. The response to the survey question 'Is water becoming an increasingly important location factor?'

| industry group | % of firms giving answer yes | size group (number of employees) | % of firms giving answer yes |
|---|---|---|---|
| food | 47.2% | 15– 49 | 12.5% |
| drink | 62.5% | 50– 99 | 25.8% |
| clothing | 25.0% | 100–199 | 39.4% |
| leather | 100 % | 200–299 | 27.8% |
| timber | 0 % | 300–499 | 33.3% |
| paper | 59.1% | 500–999 | 34.8% |
| printing | 0 % | 1000+ | 65.0% |
| chemicals | 32.0% | | |
| plastics | 36.4% | | |
| non-metallic minerals | 20.0% | | |
| mechanical engineering | 23.1% | | |
| precision engineering | 40.0% | | |

true of firms employing over 1000 persons, and for manufacturers in the paper, leather, drink and food groups. Most of these firms have in mind the increasing difficulty of finding abstraction sites producing adequate quantities or qualities of water. It would appear that although water will increase in absolute importance it will not increase relative to the other location factors. This probably reflects the increasing difficulty experienced by firms in finding a suitable piece of land for which planning permission is available and also it reflects the increasing problems faced by firms in satisfying their derived demands for suitably qualified labour.

## Conclusion

In this chapter an attempt has been made to predict the factors which will determine the future consumption of water by individual firms, although there are problems associated with this due to the use of cross-sectional data. It is believed, however, that the forecasts can be used as guide lines by planning and water authorities when considering the applications of manufacturers to locate/relocate or extend an existing plant's capacity within their area of jurisdiction. An attempt has also been made to forecast the future growth rate of industrial water consumption. If the future rate of growth is similar to that experienced over the last 10 years, it would appear that an increase in total industrial water of approximately 2% per annum will occur in the south east. There is, however, some evidence that firms *expect* to decrease their rate of increase in consumption to an average of 0.8% per annum. This does, however, only apply to existing firms, and no allowance is made for firms still to be established. From these forecasts it would appear that net consumption is unlikely to increase by the 4% per annum figure used by the Water Resources Board Technical Committee on *Water Resources in South East England*. There is, therefore, a danger of developing capacity before it is required, and this is especially important in view of the rapid improvements in the technology and economics of desalination (64). The final topic considered in this chapter is the possible future importance of water supply as a location factor. It seems that any impact on regional patterns of location will only occur in the long-run if at all, and it has also been found that little evidence exists to suggest that the availability of water facilities will increase in relative importance in the locational decisions of firms. Certainly no observable changes in industrial location will appear if there is an over development of water capacity.

# Chapter 7

# Summary

The discussion in the preceding chapters can be briefly summarized as
follows:—

1  Knowledge on industrial water usage in Britain is very slight, and
therefore, it is proposed to fill in some of the gaps in our information by
surveying a random sample of manufacturers in south east England. The
collected data will be analysed by the use of least squares regression,
mapping and frequency distributions.

2  In physical terms there is no shortage of water as more is always
available at a price. Economic limits to supply do exist, however, and
manufacturers are in competition with other water users for the available
economic supplies. Competition for water is best resolved by allocating the
resource until the marginal value of the last unit *consumed* by each
competitor is equated, and to do this it is necessary to introduce marginal
cost pricing (marginal costs being measured in opportunity cost terms).
The optimal and the actual allocative procedures do not coincide. In all
probability this results in too many resources being expended to provide
water supply facilities, and too much water being devoted to domestic and
agricultural uses, and to effluent and sewage dilution.

3  Manufacturers normally *purchase* water for staff hygiene and boiler
feed purposes; while many firms requiring cooling or process water own
private abstraction sites. In terms of the quantity of water taken, private
abstraction is by far the most important source of industrial water.

   The spatial patterns of metered water use in south east England appear
to be influenced by three factors, the density of manufacturing
employment, the relative position of manufacturing in the employment
structure of an area, and the type of industry present. In the spatial
pattern produced by private abstractors, the most noticeable feature is the
clustering of abstraction sites along the water courses in close proximity to
London.

   When an attempt was made to determine which factors caused the wide
variation between firms in the quantity of water used, it was found that
tonnage of raw material inputs and the number of persons employed were
the best explanatory variables. Levels of explanation and significance were
low, however, until the firms were divided into industry groups.

4   Intra-industry variation in the level of water usage was best explained by the raw material inputs and the level of employment in the individual firms. The price of metered water was also significantly related to the quantity of water purchased, and firms in most industry groups appear to have elastic demands for water.

5   A distinction must be made between 'spatial' and 'behavioural' theories of industrial location. The former is concerned with the factors which influence the aggregate patterns of industrial distribution and growth, whereas the latter deals with those factors that determine the locational decisions of individual business managers. The same factors need not be important in both types of theory.

Water supply and effluent disposal facilities are unlikely to play any part in a 'spatial' theory, as they contribute little to differential inter-regional development. While the factor must be considered in a 'behavioural' theory, it is only a critical locational consideration for a few business managers. However, it is important to note that large firms, employing over 1000 persons, ranked water higher than did smaller firms. Water achieved its greatest locational importance during the nineteenth century, when the public supply industry was not fully developed.

6   When the regressions on the quantity of water used produced high levels of explanation and significance, it was possible to use the best-fit equation forms to forecast future demands for water from individual firms. Although there are problems associated with forecasting from cross-sectional data, the equations should provide water engineers and planners with a *guide* to the possible future consumption of new or expanding firms.

Over the past 10 years manufacturers in the 'study area' have expanded their water usage by approximately 2% per annum, but many plant managers expect this rate of increase to decrease sharply during the next 10 years. If the expectations of the managers are correct there is a danger of the water industry developing surplus capacity.

There is no evidence that water supply will increase in importance as a factor in the regional distribution of industry, certainly any impact will only become apparent in the long-run future. It would also seem likely that water will remain a relatively minor factor in the locational decisions of business managers, although those firms requiring private abstraction water may have greater difficulty in finding a suitable site.

# Appendix A

# Industry group response rates

| Column 1 | Column 2 | Column 3 | Column 4 | Column 5 | Column 6 |
|---|---|---|---|---|---|
| industry group | total population of firms | sample size | number of usable responses | response rate | number of respondents answering part two of survey |
| food | 211 | 35 | 19 | 54% | 17 |
| drink | 82 | 30 | 9 | 30% | 9 |
| clothing and textiles | 313 | 40 | 14 | 35% | 5† |
| leather and fur | 47 | 10 | 7 | 70% | 4† |
| furniture and timber | 414 | 40 | 14 | 35% | 7† |
| paper and products | 215 | 90 | 31 | 33% | 22 |
| printing | 406 | 10 | 8 | 80% | 4† |
| plastics and rubber | 259 | 40 | 19 | 46% | 11 |
| chemicals | 487 | 140 | 61 | 44% | 50 |
| non-metallic minerals | 250 | 45 | 18 | 40% | 15 |
| metals and products | 642 | 45 | 25 | 56% | 13 |
| mechanical engineering | 1129 | 30 | 13 | 40% | 7 |
| precision engineering | 1190 | 45 | 15 | 30% | 8 |
| total | 5645 | 600* | 253 | 43% | 172 |

*the figure of 600 was reduced to 585 by non-replacement of service or warehousing firms towards the end of the survey period
†sub-groups combined into 'other' group to obtain sufficient observations in the quantity regressions

# Appendix B

# The industrial survey questionnaire

LONDON SCHOOL OF ECONOMICS AND POLITICAL SCIENCE
SURVEY ON INDUSTRIAL WATER SUPPLY

Please '✓' or
put numbers
where
applicable. If
'nil' please
put '0'.

NUMBER: | 001 |

HOW MANY PLANTS ARE THERE IN YOUR FIRM?:

Address of plant to which this return refers: (Main plant in the south east)

## Section A. General information

1 When was your firm (or your main plant) located on its present site?

2 Please number (1 to 8) the following factors in the order of their importance in the location of your plant. In column A rank them in the order that they affected the actual past locational decision. In column B assume that the decision must be remade today and enter the changed ranking, if any.

| factors | column A past decision | column B present decision |
|---|---|---|
| a labour (skill, cost, good labour relations) | | |
| b land (cost, flatness, room for expansion, suitable building already exists) | | |
| c raw materials/power/ or components (nearness to, cost of) | | |
| d market (nearness to, growth potential of) | | |
| e transport network | | |
| f water supply & effluent disposal | | |
| g accident (founder's birthplace, etc.) | | |
| h other (please specify) | | |

3   What proportion of your TOTAL COSTS are made up by each
    of the following?:

        a   raw materials/components:         %
        b   labour:         %
        c   power:         %
        d   transport costs:         %
        e   rent and rates:         %
        f   other (please specify):         %

                                                  100%

4   How many <u>TONS</u> of raw materials/components do you use
    per YEAR?:

5   How many persons are employed in your plant?:

### Section B. Water supply

1   Source of water: a  Local water undertaking:
                   Quantity per year in 1,000 gals:
                   Cost per 1,000 gals:

                b  Own supplies:
                   1  Ground water (wells, bores, etc.)
                       Quantity per year in 1,000 gals:
                       Cost per 1,000 gals:
                   2  Surface water:
                       Quantity per year in 1,000 gals:
                       Cost per 1,000 gals:
                   Is this surface water from:  Stream
                                              Tidewater
                                              Other
                                            (please specify)

                c  Any other source (please specify)
                   Quantity per year in 1,000 gals:
                   Cost per 1,000 gals:

2   Over the last 10 years has your average total consumption
    per year been:

        a  Increasing:
        b  Decreasing:
        c  Broadly stable:
        If changing, by what percentage per year?:     %

3   Do you anticipate a *future*:
        a  Increase:
        b  Decrease:
        c  Broadly stable:
        If changing, by what percentage per year?:     %

4    If you have your own supplies, have you been refused
     permission to extend them?

                                        YES:
                                        NO:

     Will the new licensing of abstractions result in
                    a    A decrease in the amount of water
                         used:
                                        YES:
                                        NO:
                    b    A cutting down of any future
                         increase:
                                        YES:
                                        NO:

5    What are your costs per 1,000 gals of treating?:
                    a    water from your own supplies:
                    b    from the local water undertaking:

6    Are these costs of treatment per 1,000 gals IN REAL TERMS:
                    a    Increasing:
                    b    Decreasing:
                    c    Stable:
          If changing, by what percentage per year?                    %

7    If the costs of treating your own supplies are increasing
     is this due to:
                    a    Increased pollution of ground water:
                    b    Increased pollution of surface water:
                    c    Increased cost of equipment:
                    d    Increasingly stringent needs:
                    e    Other (please specify):

8    Would you use a special non-potable supply of water if
     your local water undertaking provided one at a lower price?
                                        YES:
                                        NO:

9    For what purposes do you use water?
                    a    Cooling:                                      %
                    b    Washing of material:                         %
                    c    In process:                                  %
                    d    Boiler feed:                                 %
                    e    Sanitation:                                  %
                    f    Other (please specify):                      %

10   What importance had water QUANTITY in the location of
     your plant?
                    a    Crucial:
                    b    Significant:
                    c    Minor:
                    d    No importance:

What importance had water QUALITY in the location of
your plant?

    a   Crucial:

    b   Significant:

    c   Minor:

    d   No importance:

11  Is water becoming increasingly important in the location
of your industry due to the increased competition for
supplies?

                                   YES:

                                   NO:

12  If water increased in price by 100% would you?

    a   Pay the increment:

    b   Recycle:

    c   Move to area with cheaper supplies:

    d   Change process to use less water:

    e   Other (please specify):

### Section C. Effluent disposal

1  How do you dispose of your effluent?

    a   into river or the sea:

    b   into local authority sewers:

2  Do you treat effluent before disposal?

                                     YES:

                                   NO:

3  If yes, what are your treatment cost per 1,000 gals?:

Are these costs IN REAL TERMS

    a   Increasing:

    b   Decreasing:

    c   Broadly stable:

4  Has the increased control over pollution resulting from the
Rivers (Prevention of Pollution) Act, 1951-61 increased
your costs?

                                   YES:

                                   NO:

If yes, are you  a  prepared to pay the increment:

                b  considering moving your plant to an
area of less stringent requirements:

                c  considering changing your process
to produce less effluent:

                d  other (please specify):

5  What importance had the ease and cheapness of effluent
   disposal in the location of your plant?

        a   Crucial:

        b   Significant:

        c   Minor:

        d   No importance:

May I telephone you for an appointment to visit your plant?

                                       YES:

                                       NO:

Your comments and amplifications, please.

**THANK YOU**

# Bibliography<sup>*</sup>

1  Allan, R. G. D., *Statistics for Economists,* Tenth impression, London, Hurchinson University Library, 1960.

2  American Water Resources Association, *Hydata,* An International Review of the contents of periodicals in the field of water resources, Vol 1 Jan. 1965, monthly.

3  Amoss, L. Harold and Rona K. McNickle, eds., *Land and Water: planning for economic growth,* Selected papers of Western Resources Conference, 1961, University of Colorado Press, 1962.

4  Australian Academy of Science, *Water Resources: Use and Management,* proceedings of a symposium held at Canberra, 1963, Melbourne University Press, 1964.

5  Balchin, W. G. V., 'The Nation's Water Supply', *Geography* 42, 3, 1957, pp 149-59

6  Balchin, W. G. V., 'Water Use Survey', *Geographical Journal* 126, 4, 1958, pp 476-94.

7  Barnes, J. R., 'Water for United States Industry', *Resources for Freedom,* V, June 1952, Washington D.C.

8  Baumol, William Jack, *Business Behaviour, Value and Growth,* New York, Macmillan, 1959.

9  Baxter, George, 'Preservation of fish life, amenities and facilities for recreation', in Institution of Civil Engineers, *Conservation of Water Resources in the United Kingdom,* London, Institution of Civil Engineers, 1963, pp 60-8.

10  Baxter, R. E. and R. Rees, 'Analysis of Industrial Electricity Demand', *Economic Journal,* June, 1968, pp 277-298.

11  Best, Thomas D. and Robert C. Smith, 'Water in Areal Industrial Development, *Battelle Technical Revue,* Vol 6, II, 1957, pp 3-8.

*In the text each reference is refered to by the number given to it in this bibliography. Where appropriate a page or chapter reference is also given. Most of the books and articles listed here are referred to in the text, although there are a number of more general references, which have contributed to some of the views expressed in the monograph, but have not been acknowledged individually.

12    Bilham, Ernest George, *The Climate of the British Isles,* London, 1938.

13    Bird, P. A. and C. I. Jackson, 'The Water Cure', British Waterworks Association *Journal,* XLVIII, 414, 1966, pp 171-8.

14    Bird, P. A. and C. I. Jackson, 'Economic Methods of Charging for Water', British Waterworks Association *Journal,* XLVIII, 419, 1966, pp 614-28

15    Bird, P. A. and C. I. Jackson, 'Economic Charges for Water' in *Essays in the Theory and Practice of Pricing,* Readings in Political Economy, 3, London, The Institute of Economic Affairs, 1967.

16    Boulding, Kenneth E., 'The Economist and the Engineer. Economic Dynamics of Water Resource Development', in Smith, Stephen and Emery Neal Castle, eds., *Economics and Public Policy in Water Resource Development,* Ames, Iowa, Iowa State University Press, 1964, pp 82-92.

17    Bowen, William, 'Water shortage is a frame of mind', *Fortune Magazine,* April 1965, pp 111-98.

18    Bower, Blair T., 'The Economics of Industrial Water Utilization', in Kneese, Allan V. and Stephen C. Smith, eds., *Water Research,* Baltimore, John Hopkins Press, 1966, pp 143-74.

19    Britton, John Nigel Haskings, *The Bristol Industrial Region,* Typescript, Ph.D. (London), 1966

20    Brown, Phelps-E. H. and J. Wiseman, *A Course in Applied Economics,* 2nd edition, London, Pitman and Sons, 1962

21    Clark, D., 'Thermal Power Generation', in Institution of Civil Engineers, *Conservation of Water Resources in the United Kingdom,* London, Institution of Civil Engineers, 1963, pp 43-51.

22    Clawson, Marion, *Methods of measuring the Demand for and Value of Outdoor Recreation,* Resources for the Future Reprint Series 10, Washington D.C. Resources for the Future inc., 1959.

23    Cohen, Kalman J. and Richard Michael Cyert, *Theory of the Firm,* New York, Prentice Hall, 1965.

24    Colin, Andrew, *The Multiple Variate Counter* (M.V.C.), London, University of London Institute of Computer Science, 1964.

25  Craine, Lyle E., *Water Resources Management in England and Wales,* Draft, Typescript.

26  Cyert, Richard Michael and James Gardner March, eds., *A Behavioural Theory of the Firm,* New York, Prentice Hall, 1963.

27  *Daily Mail,* 'Drought Cuts House-Building', leader by Peter Whaley, Property Correspondent, Tuesday, December 21, 1965, p 1.

28  Davis, J. F. and R. F. Baker, 'The Economic Geography of Lower Thameside', in K. M. Clayton, ed., *Guide to London Excursions,* London, London School of Economics, 1964, pp 68-71.

29  Durbin, J. and G. S. Watson, 'Testing for Serial Correlation in Least-Squares Regression' pts 1 and 11, *Biometrika,* 37, p 409 and 38, p 159, 1950 and 1951.

30  Durfor, Charles N. and Edith Becker, *Public Water Supplies of 100 Largest Cities in the United States,* U.S. Government Printing Office, 1962.

31  Eckstein, Otto, *Water-Resource Development: The Economics of Project Evaluation,* Cambridge, Mass., Harvard University Press, 1961.

32  Embleton, C. and A. B. Mountjoy, 'Geomorphology and Industry in part of the Middle Thames Valley' in *Guide to London Excursions,* London School of Economics, 1964, pp 88-92.

33  Essex River Authority, Licence of Right *Register,* unpublished.

34  Ezekiel, Mordecai and Karl A. Fox, *Methods of Correlation and Regression Analysis,* Third edition, New York, John Wiley and Sons Inc., 1963.

35  Federation of British Industries, *Control of water in England and Wales,* F.B.I. Handbook, 1964

36  Florence, Philip Sargant, *Post-War Investment, Location and Size of Plant,* Cambridge, University Press, 1962.

37  Fox, Irving K., 'We can solve our water problems', *Water Resources Research* 2, 1966, 4, pp 617-23.

38  Fox, Irving K. and Orris C. Herfindahl, *Attainment of efficiency in satisfying demands for water resources,* Resources for the Future

Reprint Series, No 46, Washington D.C., Resources for the Future Inc., 1964.

39 Freund, John Ernest and Frank Jefferson Williams, *Modern Business Statistics*, London, Pitman, 1959.

40 Garfield, Paul J. and Wallace F. Lovejoy, *Public Utility Economics*, New York, Prentice Hall, 1964.

41 Gibson, J. R., 'Effluent Disposal and Industrial Geography', *Geography*, 200, XLIII, 2, 1958, pp 128-30.

42 Gottlieb, M., 'Urban Domestic Demand for Water', *Land Economics*, 39, 2, 1963, pp 204-10.

43 Graham, Jack B. and Meredith F. Burrill, eds., *Water for Industry*, Publication No 45, American Association for the Advancement of Science, Washington D.C., A.A.A.S., 1956.

44 Greenhut, M. L., *Plant Location in Theory and in Practice*, Chapel Hill, University of North Carolina Press, 1956.

45 Greenhut, M. L. and M. R. Colberg, *Factors in the Location of Florida Industry*. Florida State University Studies, No 36, De Land, Florida State University Press, 1962.

46 Gregory, S., 'Rainfall Studies and Water Supply Problems in the British Isles', *The Advancement of Science*, XIII, 50, 1957, pp 347-51.

47 Gregory, S., 'Water Supply Maps in England and Wales', *Town Planning Review*, XXVIII, 2, 1957, pp 145-63.

48 Gregory, S., 'The Contribution of the Uplands to the Public Water Supply of England and Wales', Institute of British Geographers, Publication No 25, *Transactions and Papers*, 1958, pp 153-65.

49 Gregory, S., 'Conurbation Water Supplies in Great Britain', *Journal of Town Planning Institute*, 44, 9, 1958, pp 250-3

50 Haggett, P., 'Trend Surface Analysis in Inter-Regional Comparison', University of Bristol *Seminar Paper A. No 3.*, University of Bristol, Geography Department, 1967.

51 Hart, Judith A., *Demand for Water by Manufacturing Industry in South-East England*, M. Phil. Thesis (London) June 1968, typescript.

52  Hirshleifer, Jack, James P. De Haven and Jerome W. Milliman, *Water Supply: Economics, Technology and Policy,* Chicago, University of Chicago Press, 1960.

53  Hoover, Edgar Malone, *The Location of Economic Activity,* New York, McGraw-Hill, 1948.

54  Hopthrow, H. E., 'Utilization of Water in Industry' in *Conservation of Water Resources in the United Kingdom,* London, The Institution of Civil Engineers, 1963.

55  Howe, Charles W., 'Broad Horizons in Water Resouce Planning and Investment', *Water Resources Research,* 2, 4, 1966, pp 843-7.

56  Ilersic, Alfred Roman, *Statistics,* London, H.F.L., 1959.

57  Institute of Municipal Treasurers and Accountants, *Water Statistics,* 1962-3, 1963-4, 1965-6, London, Inst. of Mun. Treas. and Accountants.

58  Institution of Civil Engineers, *Conservation of Water Resources in the United Kingdom,* Proceedings of a Symposium, Oct. 1962, London, Institution of Civil Engineers, 1963.

59  Institution of Water Engineers, *Water Engineers' Handbook,* 1965, Guardian Technical Journals Ltd., London, 1965.

60  International Water Supply Association, *Methods of Charging for Water* No 9, E. Sherman Chase, ed., 3rd Congress of the Association, 1955, pp 711-96.

61  International Water Supply Association, *Water Metering and Water Meters* No 3, S. P. Hutton, ed., 5th Congress of the Association, 1961, pp 197-322.

62  Jackson, C. I. and P. A. Bird, 'Water Meters, Why Not?', *New Society,* 142, 17th June 1965, pp 11-3.

63  Johnson, R. W. M., *Public Utility Pricing: Municipal Water Supply in Salisbury, Southern Rhodesia,* Technical Paper in Agricultural Economics, No 14, University of Rhodesia and Nyasaland, 1965.

64  Johnson, Timothy, 'Britain's lead in making sea water sweet', *Statist,* 16th July, 1965.

65  Johnston, J., *Econometric Methods,* New York, McGraw-Hill, 1963.

66  Kalton, Graham, *Introduction to Statistical Ideas for Social Scientists,* London, Chapman and Hall, 1966.

67  Katona, George and James N. Morgan, 'The Quantitative Study of Factors determining Business Decisions', *Quarterly Journal of Economics,* LXVI, 1952, pp 67-90.

68  Kent River Authority. Licence of Right *Register,* unpublished.

69  Key, A., 'River Pollution and its Control: Present and Future', *Annual Conference of River Boards Association,* 1960, p 10.

70  Klein, Lawrence Robert, *A Textbook of Econometrics,* Evanston, Row, 1953.

71  Kneese, Allan V., *Water Pollution: Economic Aspects and Research Needs,* Washington, Resources for the Future Inc., 1962.

72  Kneese, Allen V., *The Economics of Regional Water Quality Management,* Baltimore, Resources for the Future, John Hopkins Press, 1964.

73  Kneese, Allen V.,and Stephen C. Smith, eds., *Water Research,* Baltimore, John Hopkins Press, 1966.

74  Knight, Charles and Company, *The Public Health Acts 1875-1962,* London, Knight, 1963.

75  Kompass Register Ltd., *Kompass Register 1965.* Croydon, Kompass Register Ltd., 1966.

76  Krutilla, John V. and Otto Eckstein, *Multiple Purpose River Development,* Baltimore, R.F.F., John Hopkins Press, 1958.

77  Lee Conservancy Catchment Board, Licence of Right *Register,* unpublished.

78  Lipsey, Richard George, *An Introduction to Positive Economics,* London, Weidenfeld and Nicolson, 1963.

79  London School of Economics Computer Unit, A Library programme, *G.E.N.S.T.E.P.*

80  London School of Economics Computer Unit, A Library programme, *M.R.E.G.I.*

81  London School of Economics Computer Unit, A Library programme, *S.P.C.N.T.*

82  Luttrell, William Fownes, *Factory Location and Industrial Movement,* 2 vols, London, National Institute of Economic and Social Research, 1962.

83  Maass, Arthur Aaron, *Design of Water-Resource Systems,* London, Macmillan, 1962.

84  *Manual of British Water Engineering Practice,* 3rd edition, London, 1961.

85  March, James Gardner and Herbert Alexander Simon, *Organizations,* New York, Wiley, 1959 and 1966.

86  McKean, Roland Neely, *Efficiency in Government through Systems Analysis,* New York, Wiley, 1958.

87  McMillan, T. E. Junior, 'Why Manufacturers choose Plant Locations *vs* Determinants of Plant Locations', *Land Economics,* 41, 3, 1965, pp 239-46.

88  Milliman, J. W., 'Welfare Economics and Resource Development', in Amoss and McNickle, eds., *Land and Water,* University of Colorado Press, 1962, pp 183-90.

89  Moser, Claus Adolf, *Survey Methods in Social Investigation,* London, Heineman, 1961.

90  Ostrom, Vincent A., 'The Role of Public and Private Agencies in Planning the use of Water Resources', in Amoss and McNickle, eds., *Land and Water,* University of Colorado Press, 1962, pp 29-50.

91  Pailing, Katharine, 'The River Thames from Central London to Greenwich', in *Guide to London Excursions,* London School of Economics, 1964, pp 53-9.

92  Penman, H. L., 'Evaporation over the British Isles', *Journal of the Institute of Water Engineers,* 8, 1954, pp 415-28.

93  Pugh, Norman J., 'Water Supply' in *Conservation of Water Resources in the United Kingdom,* London, Inst. of Civil Engineers, 1963, pp 8-12.

94  Raffety, S. R., 'Introductory Survey' in *Conservation of Water Resources in the United Kingdom,* Institution of Civil Engineers Symposium in 1962, London, Institution of Civil Engineers, 1963, pp 4-8.

95  Rees, Judith A., *Spatial and Behavioural Theories of Industrial Location*, 1968, Manuscript.

96  Renshaw, Edward F., *Toward Responsible Government*, Chicago, Idyia Press, 1957.

97  Ronalds, A. R., 'The Industrial Use of Water' in Australian Academy of Science, *Water Resources: Use and Management*, Canberra Symposium 1963, Melbourne, University Press, 1964, pp 55-60.

98  Sant, Morgan E. C., *Private Communication*, information obtained from work on industrial employment, to be submitted for the degree of Ph.D. University of London.

99  Sealy, K. R., 'Land use on the Thames terraces and adjoining country in West Middlesex and Buckinghamshire', in *Guide to London Excursions*, London School of Economics, 1964, pp 83-7.

100  Sharp, D. H., 'The effects of the Water Resources Act on industry', The River Board's Association *Yearbook* 12, 1964, p 59.

101  Simon, Herbert Alexander, 'A Behavioural Model of Rational Choice', *Quarterly Journal of Economics*, 69, 1952, pp 99-118.

102  Simon, Herbert Alexander, 'Theories of Decision Making in Economics and Behavioural Science', *American Economic Review*, 49, 1959.

103  Sleeman, John F., 'Economics of Water Supply', *Scottish Journal of Political Economy* II, 1955, pp 231-45.

104  Smith, Stephen C. and Emery N. Castle, eds., *Economics and Public Policy in Water Supply Development*, Ames, Iowa, Iowa State University Press, 1964.

105  Speight, H., '*Private Communication* on paper "Economic Methods of Charging for Water" presented at B.W.A. Annual Summer Meeting—June 1966', Reading, Water Resources Board, 1347/30/6/66, Typescript, 1966.

106  Spiegal, Murray R., *Theory and Problems of Statistics*, New York, Schaum Publishing Company, 1961, p 191.

107  Sporck, J. A., *L'activite industrielle dans la région liégeoise: étude de géographie économique*, Liège, Thone, 1957.

108   Starkie, David Nicholas Martin, *An inquiry into certain aspects of commercial road traffic generation by manufacturing industry*, M.Sc.(Econ) London, typescript, 1966.

109   Starkie, David Nicholas Martin, *Traffic and Industry*, London School of Economics, 1967.

110   Stern, Walter M., 'Water Supply in Britain: The Development of a Public Service', *British Waterworks Association Journal*, Vol 37, 1955, p 14.

111   Stevens, Joe B., 'Recreation Benefits from Water Pollution Control', *Water Resources Research*, 2, 2, 1966, pp 167-82.

112   Sussex River Authority, Licence of Right *Register*, unpublished.

113   Thames Conservancy Catchment Board, Licence of Right *Register*, unpublished.

114   Thames Conservancy Catchment Board, *Charging Scheme* under Section 58 of the Water Resources Act, 1963, Conservators of the River Thames, 12th February, 1968.

115   Twyman, Paul Hadleigh, *Industrial Location in East Kent with special reference to factory relocation and branch plant establishment*, M.Sc.(Econ) thesis, London, unpublished, 1967.

116   United Kingdom Government, *Water Act 1945*, London, H.M.S.O., 1945.

117   United Kingdom Government, *Rivers Act 1951*, London, H.M.S.O., 1951

118   United Kingdom Government, *Rivers Act 1961*, London, H.M.S.O., 1961

119   United Kingdom Government, *Water Resources Act 1963*, London, H.M.S.O., 1963.

120   United Kingdom Government, *Water Conservation in England and Wales, Cmnd. 1693,* London, H.M.S.O., 1962.

121   United Kingdom Government: Ministry of Agriculture, Fisheries and Food, *The calculation of irrigation need*, Technical Bulletin No 4, 2nd edition, London, H.M.S.O., 1960.

122 United Kingdom Government: Central Statistical Office, *Standard Industrial Classification*, 2nd edition, H.M.S.O., 1958.

123 United Kingdom Government: Ministry of Housing and Local Government, *Report 1957*, presented to Parliament May 1958, Cmnd. 419, London, H.M.S.O., 1958.

124a United Kingdom Government: Ministry of Housing and Local Government: Central Advisory Water Committee: Sub-Committee on Growing Demand for Water, *1st Report*, London, H.M.S.O., 1959.
 b *2nd Report*, London, H.M.S.O., 1960.
 c *Final Report*, London, H.M.S.O., 1962.

125 United Kingdom Government: Ministry of Housing and Local Government: Central Advisory Water Committee: Sub-Committee on Water Charges, *Report*, October 1962, London, H.M.S.O., 1963.

126 United Kingdom Government: Ministry of Housing and Local Government, *South East Study 1961-1981*, London, H.M.S.O., 1961.

127 United Kingdom Government, Ministry of Land and Natural Resources: Water Resources Board, *Water Supplies in South East England*, London, H.M.S.O., 1966.

128 United Nations: Department of Economic and Social Affairs, *Water for Industrial Use*, U.N. II. B. 1958. 1.

129 United States Government, Bureau of the Census, *Census of Manufactures*, 1958, Vol 1, Summary Statistics, Chapter XI, 'Industrial Water Use', Washington D.C., United States Government Printing Office, 1961.

130 United States Government: Geological Survey, *Water Supply Paper 1299*, Washington D.C., United States Government Printing Office, 1955.

131 United States Government, Presidents Material Policy Commission (Paley Commission), *Resources for Freedom Vol 1*, Washington D.C., United States Government Printing Office, 1952.

132 Warford, J. J., 'Water Requirements. The Investment Decision in the Water Supply Industry', *The Manchester School*, Jan. 1966, pp 87-112.

133 Warren, K., 'Locational Problems of the Scottish Iron and Steel

Industry since 1760', part 2, *Scottish Geographic Magazine*, 81, 2, pp 87-103.

134 *Water and Water Engineering*, 'Price levels', editorial April 1966, pp 137-8.

135 White, Gilbert, 'Industrial Water Use', *Geographical Review*, 1960, pp 412-30

136 White, Langdon C., 'Water, a neglected factor in the literature of Iron and Steel', *Geographical Review*, 1957, pp 463-89.

137 Wisdom, Allen Sidney, *The Law on the Pollution of Waters*, London, Shaw, 1956.

138 Wisdom, Allen Sidney, *The Law of Rivers and Watercourses*, London, Shaw, 1962.

139 Witherick, M. E., 'Aspects of Land Use in the Lower Lea Valley', in *Guide to London Excursions*, London School of Economics, 1964, pp 45-50.

140 Wollman, Nathaniel, ed., *The Value of Water in Alternative Uses*, Albuquerque, University of New Mexico Press, 1962.

# Notes

# Chapter 1

1. A complete bibliography can be found at the end of the monograph on pages 169–179. In the text a reference number and where appropriate the page or chapter number will be given.

2. Malvern Urban District Council are exceptional in that they provide a metered water supply for most domestic, as well as commercial and industrial consumers. (62 pp 11-3.)

3. An industrial directory which lists most commercial, and industrial concerns in Britain by industry group and by location.

4. A complete list of firms in the Medway towns was obtained from D. M. Starkie, who conducted a survey of this area for his work on traffic generation (108 and 109). The complete population of firms in Bishop's Stortford and East Grinstead was established by field inspection and interviewing.

5. If the Kompass *Register* were used to conduct a similar survey in another region of Britain it is possible that a relatively large number of branch plants would be omitted from the sample frame; these branches would have the parent company located in south east England.

6. It was assumed that due to basic similarities in technology industry groups with like water using characteristics in the United States would also have similar characteristics in Britain.

7. To obtain the American standard deviations the formula

$$SD = \sqrt{\left[ \sum_{i=1}^{n} \frac{(x_i - \bar{x})^2}{n} \right]}$$

was used where:—
$x_i$ = water consumption of the 'i' th minimum list heading
$\bar{x}$ = mean water consumption for the whole industry group
$n$ = total number of minimum list headings in the industry group
(39 p 85)

8. The following formula **was** used to calculate the number of firms to sample in each industry group:—

$$\frac{n_h}{n} = \frac{N_h S_h}{\Sigma N_h S_h}$$

where: $n_h$ = number of firms to be sampled in the 'h'th group
: $n$ = total number of firms to be sampled
: $N_h$ = number of firms in the 'h'th group in the total population
: $S_h$ = standard deviation of firms in the 'h'th group in the total population.

9 The Lee Catchment Board and the Thames Conservancy Catchment Boards have the same functions as a river authority conferred by order under Section 125 of the *Water Resources Act* (p 123).

10 The counties of Middlesex and London have now been incorporated into the Greater London Council Area, established in 1965.

# Chapter 2

1 Elasticity of demand is defined at the responsiveness of demand to price changes. $= \dfrac{\% \text{ change in quantity}}{\% \text{ change in price}}$ (78 p 108)

2 Opportunity costs are costs measured in terms of foregone alternatives; for example the cost of a storage reservoir may be a hospital or school (78 pp 60-1).

3 Indivisibilities exist when it is not possible to increase the scale of production by very small amounts. Plant and equipment must be provided in 'lumps'.

4 Phelps-Brown and Wiseman were discussing the general principles of marginal cost pricing. For an explicit consideration of marginal cost pricing in the water industry see Bird and Jackson, 1967 (14), and Warford (132).

5 The exact size of this proportion is still open to question—see discussion Chapter 3.

6 There are, however, some local authority undertakings which aim to incur a loss that is subsidized from the general rates fund, or conversely, which treat water supply as a revenue raiser (57 column 22).

7 Unmeasured supplies also include the undertakings pipeline losses. In the south east these losses are usually 5% to 20% of the total water supplied, and therefore the income from unmeasured supplies is deflated.

8  Section 49, part 3 of the 3rd Schedule states that premises supplied on a meter shall be supplied at a charge which is subject "to a minimum annual charge equal to the annual amount which would be payable by way of water rate for a supply of water for domestic purposes furnished to the premises in question".

# Chapter 3

1  It was found in the test interviews that the cost of abstracted water was invariably underestimated. Firms often ignored treatment costs, the capital costs of pumping and treatment equipment, and the labour charges. This underestimation does not, however, make the true cost of abstraction anywhere near that of purchased water.

2  The figure must be viewed with caution as unmetered firms could only *estimate* their consumption.

3  Let $x$ *mgd* = Total public supply
Total industrial supply = $(1 + 0.38)x$
Therefore proportion of total industrial supply purchased from public undertakings = $0.38x/(1 + 0.38)x \times 100 = 0.38/1.38 \times 100 = 21\%$

4  It is in fact common for large abstractors to own both surface and underground sources to satisfy different quality requirements, see page 35.

5  It is now thought that it would have been possible to reduce all the data to surfaces, and then to compare statistically the various surfaces obtained (50).

6  In other words water usage by industry would only rarely vary with space (or distance) itself, rather it varies between areas because of the different characteristics of the space, which are derived from variations in population density, industrial concentration etc.

7  An 'F' test was used to establish whether the results were significant at the 0.95 level of probability.

8  The per person gallonage figure was obtained from the regression coefficient (b) (table 5 column 3) which gives the slope of the regression line for a linear relationship. As the computations were

made in 1,000 gallons, the coefficient was multiplied by 1,000 to obtain gallons per employee per annum.

9 Probability is the *long-run* relative frequency with which an event takes place. Therefore a 0.95 level of probability means in this case that in the long run there will be a negative relationship between price and quantity 95% of the time (39 pp 110-3).

10 The price elasticity of demand is defined as
– % change in quantity/% change in price
The more responsive firms are to price changes the higher the elasticity. A curve is said to be elastic if the elasticity is greater than one, and inelastic if it is less than one (78 p 112). All elasticities have a minus sign since quantity *decreases* as price *increases*.

# Chapter 4

1 Strictly these workings should be omitted from the study, as non-manufacturing units, although the firm itself may manufacture goods.

2 This claim was made by the technical manager of a large raw paper producing plant in north Kent.

3 The number of degrees of freedom is defined as the number of independent observations in the sample minus the number of population parameters which must be estimated from the sample observations (106 p 191) for an explanation of the use of this value see 39 pp 98-9.

4 No importance should be attached to the order in which these industry groups are presented.

5 An easily used measure of significance at the 0.95 level is when the regression coefficient is over 1.96 times greater than the standard error.

6 The constant term in a regression equation is the value of the dependent variable when the independent variable equals zero. (See figure 5.)

7 The equation form shown here and used elsewhere in the analysis is not the usual quadratic equation ($Q = a + bE + cE^2$), which did not produce such good levels of significance and explanation.

8 It can be seen that the level of private abstraction and total water usage increases much more rapidly as employment increases than the quantity of water purchased does (see previous paragraph).

9 Elasticity was defined on page 184, notes to Chapter 3. The responsiveness of demand to price changes varies over the demand curve, and it can be calculated for any point on the curve (78 p 125).

10 The regression equations are all mathematical descriptions of various curves showing relationships between variables. The equations and the accompanying curves are described clearly by Ezekial and Fox (34 pp 70-80).

11 The slope of a regression line derived from this equation form is calculated from the equation: slope = $b/2\sqrt{(a + bT)}$.

12 As the regression equation is $QA^2 = a + bT$; then the point where the regression line cuts the $QA$ axis = $\sqrt{(a)}$.

13 When the equation form is linear the slope of the regression line is the $b$ coefficient. This value is then multiplied by 1000 to obtain the figure in gallons.

14 This problem has been discussed in detail on page 50 chapter 3.

15 The Students 't'-test was used here to test the significance of the correlation because the regression was run on a small sample, where $n$ was less than 30 observations (39 pp 195-7).

16 A dummy variable gives a numerical value to an attribute. For example in this analysis the numbers 0 and 1 were used to denote whether a firm was a raw paper producer or a manufacturer of paper products.

17 This point has been discussed in Chapter 1, page 3 and in this chapter on pages 77 to 79.

18 Most of these firms are located within the supply area of the Metropolitan Water Board.

19 For a linear curve the slope is the regression coefficient $b$. Multiply by 1000 to obtain the figure in gallons.

20 The term multicollinearity has been defined, and its effects discussed in Chapter 3, page 49.

# Chapter 5

1 Very large concerns are increasingly engaging in inter-regional comparisons, but in the majority of firms of relatively small size no such efforts are made.

2 The model is presented in rather more detail in 'Spatial and Behavioural Theories of Industrial Location' by J. A. Rees. (95.)

3 Personal communication December 1966. Lee Conservancy Catchment Board.

4 This factor includes government planning restrictions.

5 The results are presented in greater detail and in tabular form in Hart, J. A. (now Rees) *Demand for Water by Manufacturing Industry in South East England.* M. Phil. Thesis, London 1968, pages 157-72.

6 This point has been discussed in Chapter 3 page 49.

7 Throughout this discussion it must be remembered that an *increase* in the rank given to water means that water *declines* in importance to the locational decisions of firms. Rank 1 is the one given to the most important factor and rank 8 is given to the most unimportant consideration.

8 Clothing, leather and fur firms were combined into one industry group in order to obtain sufficient degrees of freedom in the regression equations (see Chapter 4, p 96).

9 See earlier note 7 (page 185).

10 It was not possible to include tonnage of raw materials and the number of persons employed in one equation due to multicollinearity, but it was possible to include both tonnage and the proportion of labour costs as these were not significantly related.

11 The water tower proved essential as any fluctuation of pressure in the high pressure pipe automatically caused the local fire station to be called out.

12 The use of spray booths will be discussed in more detail on page 152.

13 The Durbin-Watson statistic was only 0.63 (29 part 11 p 173).

14 In this industry group the percentages of power costs and raw material costs were not correlated significantly, and therefore it was possible to use them in one model.

# Chapter 6

1 The page numbers refer back to the main discussion of the industry group in Chapter 4.

2 The figure 557,000 g.p.a. is found from the value of the constant term $a$ in the regression equation. It is, in fact, $a$ x 1000. This point is treated in greater detail in Chapter 4, pages 70-71.

3 $Q^2 = 310662811 + 15121172 \ (6)$ $\therefore Q = \sqrt{(401389843)} = 20034$
Then multiply $Q$ by 1000 to obtain the value in gallons = 20,034,000.

4 The extreme tonnage and water usage figures obtained for an oil refinery were omitted from the calculation of the slope of this regression line. See Chapter 4, pages 70-72.

5 This value is the mean tonnage of raw materials handled by the sampled food manufacturers.

6 $Q^2 = a + bT$, where $Q^2$ and $T$ are in units of 1000
$a = -5197781263$
$b = 1516781730$
Then $Q^2 = -5197781263 + 1516781730 \ (75)$
$\therefore \quad Q = \sqrt{(6178081487)}$
$\therefore \quad Q = \underline{78,600}$ multiplied by 1000 to obtain the result in gallons

7 $QA^2 = a + bT$, where $QA$ and $T$ are in units of 1000
$a = 1471831182$
$b = 756270095$
Then $QA = \sqrt{(57192088307)}$
$\therefore \quad QA = \underline{239,160}$ multiplied by 1000 to obtain the result in gallons.

8 This term was explained, and the point was considered in detail in Chapter 4, page 85.

9 $Q = a + bE$, where $Q$ is in units of 1000
$a = -3381$
$b = 131.7$
$\therefore \quad Q = \underline{64,469}$ multiplied by 1000 to obtain the figure in gallons.

10 This point has been developed in detail in Chapter 4, pages 79-181.

11 The best-fit significant regression was $\log QA = a + bT$, where
$a = 7.32$
$b = -0.07914$
$\therefore \log QA \quad = 7.32 - 0.07914 \,(T)$
$\therefore$ When $\log QA = O$, then $T = 93$ multiplied by 1000 to obtain the figure in tons.

12 $QA = a + bT$, where $QA$ and $T$ are in units of 1000
$a \quad = 202440$
$b \quad = 2011996$
$\therefore QA = 202440 + 2010996\,(50)$. Then multiply by 1000 to obtain gallonage.

13 $QA = a + bT + cD$ where $QA$ and $T$ are in units of 1000
$D$ is the 0 or 1 presence or absence dummy variable. In the case of raw paper producers $D$ is 1.
$\therefore QA = -228030 + 18427\,(50) + 814570\,(1)$
$\therefore QA = 1507890$
Multiply by 1000 to obtain the value in gallons.

14 $QA = -228030 + 18427\,(50) + 814570\,(0)$
The dummy variable in the case of paper products manufacturers is 0.
$\therefore QA = -228030 + 921350$
$\therefore QA = 593320$
Multiply by 1000 to obtain the value in gallons.

15 The mean size of the respondent firms in the group is 427 persons.

16 $Q = a + bE^2$ : where $Q$ is in 1000s
$a = 573.6$
$b = 0.02796$
$Q \quad = 573.6 + 0.02796\,(400^2)$
$\therefore Q = 5,047.2$. Multiply by 1000 to obtain figure in gallons.

17 $QA \quad = -544.18 + 2.54\,(400)$
$\therefore QA \quad = 544.18 + 1016$
$\therefore QA \quad = 472$ multiplied by 1000 to obtain the figure in gallons.

18 This is a composite group, including clothing, textile, leather, fur, furniture and printing firms.

19 $Q = a + bE^2$ where $Q$ is in units of 1000
$a \quad = 117.38$
$b \quad = 0.0147$
$Q = 117.38 + 0.0147\,(180^2)$
$Q = 599.0$ multiplied by 1000 to obtain gallonage.

20  $Q = a + bT$ where $Q$ and $T$ are in units of 1000
    $a = 87.1$
    $b = 71.14$
    $Q = 87.1 + 71.14(6)$
    $Q = 514.9$ multiply by 1000 to obtain gallonage.

21  A regression statistic is the coefficient established for sample data. A regression parameter is the coefficient of the total population.

22  It is possible that firms using a higher quantity of water than the average are employing inadequate water using equipment and the statutory undertaking could possibly use the average figures as a yardstick to promote more efficient techniques.

23  This point is discussed in detail on pages 79 to 81, Chapter 4.

24  The regression analysis (Chapter 4, pages 68 and 79) suggests that the addition of one employee to the labour force will be associated with an increased demand for purchased water by chemical firms of approximately 2,200 gallons per annum. Whereas, the demand increase for food manufacturers will be approximately 130,000 gallons. Although these exact figures may be suspect it is virtually certain that the relative position will hold.

25  These relative effects are deduced directly from the different slopes of the regression lines relating employment and the demand for water from the local undertakings in each industry group. (Chapter 4 pages 68 to 99).

26  Private communication from the works manager of one food canning plant located in south east England.

27  Personal communication from A. I. Biggs, Esq., Technical Department, Confederation of British Industry. November 1965.

28  Personal communication from J. A. Ensor, Esq., Chief Engineer, Horatio Myers & Co. Ltd.

29  This is not an impossible increase to expect when the gallonage charge on abstractions is introduced.

30  A fuller treatment of the opportunity cost concept can be seen in Chapter 2, pages 15-25.

31  It is thought that a firm will rarely offer to pay the entire cost of installing the additional capacity, as this would involve paying for the water to be used by all future consumers.

32  Private communication from the Deputy Water Engineer of the authority concerned.

# Index